Survival Tactics for
Airline Passengers

Ken Cubbin

Avionics Communications Inc.

Publisher's Cataloging-in-Publication

(Provided by Quality Books, Inc.)

Cubbin, Ken.
    Survival tactics for airline passengers / Ken Cubbin.
  -- 1st ed.
    p. cm.
    ISBN: 1-885544-16-2

1. Aeronautics--Safety measures. 2. Air travel--Safety measures. 3. Aircraft accidents--Prevention.
4. Hijacking of aircraft--Prevention. Survival after airplane accidents, etc. 6. Aeronautics, Commercial--passenger traffic. I.Title.

TL553.5.C83 2002   613.6
                          QBI02-200251

Printed in the United States of America

Avionics Communications Inc.
P.O. Box 2628, Leesburg, VA 20177 USA

Tel: 703/777-9535
Fax: 703/777-9568
E-mail: avionics@avionics.com

For a complete list of titles,
visit **www.avionics.com**

Contents

Chapter 1

The New Passenger

The day of the passive airline passenger ended September 11, 2001. Ordinary citizens on an airplane rose up, banded together and, for the first time, determined their destiny.

"Let's roll!" shouted the leader. According to cell phone messages heard on the ground, passengers had joined forces and were about to rush the assailants. But the hijacking had gone too far, ending tragically in a field near Pittsburgh when the airplane plunged to the ground.

The passengers had responded heroically, but were unwary victims of a kind of hijacker the world had never seen. Yet, Flight 93 dramatically proved that passengers have the will to fight back. In the following weeks, reports grew of retaliation in the cabin. On a flight from Los Angeles passengers ganged up on a man trying to break into the cockpit.

Airline captains, for the first time, were getting on the PA and asking passengers "to lend a hand" in case of emergency.

A flight attendant said it with simple logic;

"There were only a few hijackers (on Flight 93) and over 100 passengers. The day would have ended differently if every person threw a bag, a briefcase, a cell phone---anything---at their heads!"

FAA Responds

The new trend drew notice from the highest officials when FAA Administrator Jane Garvey said:

"The past approach has always been to cooperate with a hijacker...and keep passengers calm. Obviously, the events of September 11 have changed that."

The September attack reversed everything we knew about hijacking. For decades, "air piracy" was usually a benign event. In almost every take-over, hijackers simply wanted to be flown to another country or collect ransom money. Airlines instructed their pilots to submit to any demands and expect the episode to end peacefully on the ground.

Then the rude awakening. The September 11 assailants not only acted with speed and surprise, they wielded an ultimate weapon; suicide.

"That's how a 12th-Century leader," said one observer, "turned our technology against us."

Exploding Footwear

Six weeks later an event over the mid-Atlantic erased any doubt about the end of the passive passenger. Smelling a burning match, a flight attendant discovered a man "trying to light his shoes." She saw wires protruding from his sneaker and tried to grab them. The 6-foot-4 man shoved her against the cabin wall. She yelled for help. Passengers leaped up and fought the man back into the seat. A passenger in the row behind reached over and pulled back the man's arms. Two others grabbed his legs. Several jumped over seats to assist. Some poured water on him, another aimed a fire extinguisher at his head. Suddenly, earphone cords, seat belts, straps and leather belts appeared to restrain him. Two doctors aboard injected him with a sedative.

That quick, collective response, completely unknown before, averted a nighttime tragedy in the waters of the North Atlantic. After the airplane landed in Boston, authorities determined the man's sneakers contained enough explosives to blow a large hole in the cabin. The FBI issued a statement;

"The willingness of flight attendants and passengers to get involved helped avert a potentially dangerous situation."

As news of the event circulated, it marked the end of the timid air traveler. Increasingly, airline captains appealed for help over the PA; "Get to know your neighbor" and "Look around for anything suspicious."

Fighter Escort

One of the first official responses to September 11 was to scramble military aircraft to intercept airliners that called for help or strayed off course. On October 8, 2001, an American Airlines' flight summoned assistance when a deranged passenger tried to enter the cockpit. An F-16 fighter flew to the scene and escorted the airliner to an uneventful landing at Chicago.

Two days later aboard a Continental flight, a man alarmed flight attendants by imitating the act of cutting his throat with a plastic knife. Again, a jet fighter joined the airliner in flight. Similar assistance was given October 11, when Delta 357 made an emergency landing at Shreveport, Louisiana after a passenger handed a threatening note to a flight attendant.

It sounds comforting to be protected by an armed military jet. Maybe not, because the reality is the opposite. The rules-of-engagement are to shoot you down if terrorists take control and steer toward a populated area. A frightening prospect, true, but one that's calculated to save the greatest number of lives.

Foiling terrorists before they take control---the central theme of this book---may well prevent the tragic shoot-down or take-over of a civilian airliner.

Eluding the Metal Detector

Terrorism should be detected, experts say, before you board the airplane. Yet, with all the sophisticated technology for airports, detection may not be 100 percent. Plastic knives, for example, are the weapon of prisoners because they don't affect metal detectors. A defendant in a Los Angeles courtroom stabbed two bailiffs with a 10-inch plastic knife before he was subdued. Some razor-sharp knives are made of composites with blades that pierce steel drums.

On October, 2001 a security screener at New Orleans Airport missed a passenger with a loaded gun in his briefcase After he boarded the plane, the man realized what happened and turned it over to flight attendants. Such a lapse might be understandable if it were an isolated case. Since September 11, however, security

4

screeners under new FAA guidelines missed everything from a loaded .22 caliber pistol in a pocket to a knife hidden in a shoe.

Good Start

The time for a new passenger---informed, perceptive and ready---has arrived. Those early attempts to foil hijackers were tentative and improvised. But now we know the nature of the enemy and what it takes to fight back. And that's what this book is about.

Be Defensive-Not Lethal!

The tactics shown in this book are not intended to be lethal, but to help you subdue and restrain the perpetrators. These techniques can activate the most powerful weapon available to passengers in an airplane; the ability to band together and mount a massive response.

We look at other hazards, too. With simple techniques you can vastly improve your chance of survival in other catastrophic situations. Airplane crashes may be devastating, but you have more control over the outcome than you might suspect. Over 70 percent of passengers are not killed by the impact of a crash. Fatalities mainly occur in the minutes after the crash. Safety agencies offer scores of ways to greatly improve your chances of survival and every passenger should know them.

Even on smooth, uneventful flights there are dozens of tips, gleaned from a lifetime of flying, that can make your experience safer and more comfortable.

Chapter 2

At the Airport

Widely praised for its security, the Israeli airline El Al should be the yardstick, aviation experts say, for everyone else. Within hours of September 11, El Al was called by airlines around the world seeking advice. The year before it established a training unit for airline security agents and demand ran high.

Passengers are scrutinized intensely before they get near an El Al airplane. According to a former guard, every passenger is checked through Interpol for a criminal record before the flight. At Ben Gurion Airport, cars are examined by Uzi-carrying guards, while plainclothes officers patrol airport entrances. Overseas airports where El Al lands are also covered by Israeli guards.

Passengers checks are strict. Some people are singled out for lengthy interrogation and luggage inspection. The staff separates passengers' names into low-risk (Israeli citizens or foreign Jews), medium-risk (non-Jewish foreigners), and high-risk (anyone with an Arabic name). High-risk passengers are taken to a room for a body search and interrogation.

Guards claim they can quickly spot passengers who appear nervous---hastening to add that such draconian security prevents terrorists from placing bombs on aircraft. There have been cases of innocent passengers duped into carrying a bomb in their luggage. A woman from Ireland, for example, was unaware her Palestinian boyfriend had planted explosives in her luggage. El Al guards found the bomb during their rigorous passenger and luggage inspection.

Passenger Profiling

Singling out people who raise suspicions because of race, ethnicity, dress, age or other subjective criteria is "profiling." It's done by El Al but is a touchy subject in the United States. The American Civil Liberties Union (ACLU) vigorously objects to police profiling suspected felons based on race. When scrutinized this way, Americans often decry the practice as anathema to the nation's core values. Even random breath-testing for drunk drivers is opposed by many citizens, who say it is prejudicial. In any case, be prepared for more probing questions and personal searches when next you travel.

In 1993, a female passenger sued El Al for emotional trauma after a search. She was taken a security area , treated as high-risk, detained for more than an hour and questioned. She was touched, she said, inappropriately by a female officer. Claiming she was traumatized, she could not enjoy her vacation and required medical and psychiatric treatment. A $5-million lawsuit went through lengthy litigation until thrown out by the U.S. Supreme Court. In an 8-to-1 decision, the justices held that the Warsaw Convention governs an airline's liability for international flights and, therefore, precludes damages at the state or federal level. Justice Ruth Bader Ginsburg stated for the court, "We hold today that a passenger may not recover damages under another source of law when the convention excludes recovery."

U.S. international flights, therefore, may well profile passengers and subject them to rigorous, El Al-type security. The Supreme Court decision does not appear to apply to U.S. domestic

A plastic knife may pass unnoticed through an airport metal detector. This one, the Busse Stealth Hawk, has a 4-1/2-inch serrated blade made from a high-tech laminate. It is said to be as hard as steel, with considerable cutting power.

flights, but airlines might get around this by not revealing their profiling criteria---that is, until a disgruntled employee reveals it.

El Al's level of scrutiny, therefore, may be unworkable in the U.S. But some form of passenger profiling will undoubtedly appear despite the objections of civil libertarians.

If security personnel have any doubts regarding passenger luggage or freight, an El Al flight is delayed. The airline also does not permit baggage transfers between airlines because it might move explosive material on board. Bags from one flight to another must undergo another rigorous inspection.

This assurance would be difficult to translate to U.S. airlines because of international agreements which provide a seamless flow of passengers and luggage. Regardless of which airline operates the flight, passengers expect to check bags in at departure and pick them up at the destination with little delay. If this reverts to the old days of getting your bags and checking in again with another airline, it could severely hamper airline efficiency and commerce.

El Al won't fly unless every piece of luggage is scanned for explosives and personally claimed by each passenger. Carry-on and checked baggage are X-rayed for explosives, including the elusive liquid type. The FAA has called for scanning devices for check-in baggage at every major airport in the U.S. by the end of 2002, but this may take two or three years longer than anticipated because of high demand and long delivery time.

"Positive bag matching," where each passenger is matched to his or her luggage, may be onerous for the discount airlines. They rely on rapid turnaround as a competitive advantage. East coast carrier JetBlue began matching bags to passengers on its own, but other airlines are resisting. According to the Air Transport Association, positive bag match would not improve security because suicidal terrorists could accompany explosive-laden luggage.

El Al is probably the only airline in the world that places cargo in a decompression chamber. At least ten planes of other airlines have been blown up by terrorists with fuses triggered by altitude pressure. It is also believed El Al reinforces cargo holds to withstand bomb blasts. While the decompression chamber is

Rapiscan

This airport scanner for carry-on bags uses "Multi-Energy X-Ray" processing instead of conventional X-Rays. It provides additional information about the chemical composition of items moving through, distinguishing materials according to their atomic weight, and using different colors to classify objects on the screen.

Cargo inspection machine uses the same (X-ray) technology as smaller scanners for carry-on bags, but are physically large to accommodate cargo. The device screens for concealed weapons, explosives, narcotics and other contraband. (Rapiscan)

unlikely in the near future, U.S. airlines may yet decide to structurally beef-up cargo holds.

No one can argue El Al's success in thwarting terrorist attacks. Their interceptions include a bomb found in a German passenger's bag in Zurich in 1979. The passenger appeared nervous because he thought he had been recruited to smuggle diamonds. And there was the Irish woman with luggage seeded by explosives by her Palestinian boyfriend.

Armed Guards

Up to five armed undercover agents travel on El Al flights, usually in strategically placed aisle seats. They are often ex-soldiers with combat training. In 1970 a Palestinian hijacker was killed and another wounded by a such a guard. The U.S. has added air marshals to its security forces, as described later, but the sheer volume of flights could require thousands of marshals to protect every flight.

El Al pilots enter the cockpit and are sealed by doors of reinforced steel. They do not emerge until every passenger has deplaned at the destination. The pilots are believed to have guns in the cockpit, but the airline refuses to comment. It will also not reveal how pilots are fed and allowed access to the rest room, but it's assumed there are separate facilities accessible from the cockpit.

An Israeli official who helped design El Al's security, advised PanAm in 1987 on how to prevent terrorist attacks. PanAm rejected profiling passengers, opening bags and hiring professional security because of the cost. The following year, PanAm 103 exploded over Lockerbie, Scotland killing 270 people.

El Al is not flawless. Only after September 11 did flight attendants stop selling Swiss Army knives. Undercover air marshals can probably subdue anyone who tries a hijacking with a Swiss Army knife, but it does not make sense to sell them on board.

Security does not come cheap; it costs about $100 million per year for an airline that is tiny in comparison to its U.S. counterparts. There are about 40 flights a day, while American Airlines operates about 2,400 flights a day (pre-September 11). If U.S. airlines emulated El Al, the costs would run in the billions. So it's not a question whether security should increase, but to what degree and who will foot the bill? In a deregulated environment, the cost of security is added to the price of ticket.

Even the most stringent security may not cover every eventuality. Passengers must learn to rely on his or her wits, because safety may ultimately depend on how you react to an emergency.

Congress Acts

In November, 2001, Congress tightened security in these areas:

•The federal government will control baggage screening. Later, airports, may revert to private companies.

•Airports will scan checked luggage for explosive, biological and chemical weapons. By the end of 2002 all luggage must be screened.

•A database will be established so names on law-enforcement watch lists can be cross-checked against passenger manifests.

•Cockpit doors will be reinforced and video cameras installed in the cabin. More air marshals will be employed and a hijacking alert switch for the cabin crew will be installed.

•Pilots may be able to bear weapons in the cockpit.

•These changes will be funded by a $2.50 passenger levy each way.

Scanning for Explosives

Before September 11, the FAA installed explosives scanners in 132 of 420 airports around the country, mostly for international flights. Only about 5% of domestic flights had luggage scanning. In a fast-track upgrade program, the scanners are expected to be at every major airport by December, 2002.

Purchasing machines and integrating them into airports is time-consuming and expensive. Four machines at Geneva--- a medium-size international facility with 8 million passengers a year---took about six months.

Explosive Detection Systems (EDS)

The push to develop explosives detection came after PanAm 103 blew up over Lockerbie, Scotland in 1988. Such detection devices operate at 130 U.S. airports, with full deployment (420) by the end of 2002.

One problem with explosive detection systems at U.S. airports is that they stand apart from other systems; bags must be removed from conveyer belts, taken to another area, scanned and returned for various flights. In Geneva the machines are integrated into a conveyance so each bag is checked as it moves along the belt. Not having to be removed and replaced, the bags move with little delay. Installing similar systems in the U.S. would mean tearing down existing facilities and incorporating EDS equipment.

Screening passengers, one equipment manufacturer says, should be layered. This includes profiling, passenger demeanor, explosives trace testing, body scanning and body pat-downs. Passengers are offered a choice between a body pat-down (by a same-sex officer) or a body scan. The U.S. Customs Service uses this approach successfully.

A similar idea has been operating at Tokyo's International Airport at Narita. Their layered system does positive ID checks of

Example of an FAA-certified Explosives Detection System (EDS) is this Invision CTX 9000 Dsi. The machine handles 542 bags per hour including oversized luggage and is designed to integrate into the airport baggage handling facilities.

A computer analyzes slices of luggage views and compares them with known explosive data in its memory. If a match is found, an alarm warns the operator to determine if the threat is real.

passengers entering airport security checkpoints, X-raying luggage and carry-on baggage, body metal detection and same-sex pat-downs for passengers who set off an alarm.

Threat Image Projection (TIP)

This is a check on the security personnel. It randomly inserts images of guns, knives and bombs onto the screen which shows passenger bags moving through X-ray scanners. When an operator sees a threat, he hits a stop button. TIP flashes a congratulatory message and records the screener's performance. This keeps personnel alert and tests their skill at detecting dangerous objects. The results are stored for training.

There are several hundred TIP devices in the United States. In July 2001, the FAA announced contracts worth $120 million to purchase up to 800 machines from each vendor. Over three years, the FAA plans to replace every scanner in the country (1,200) with TIP X-ray machines.

Body Scanners

Used in such high-security applications as prisons, the body scanner resembles a refrigerator. You stand in front of the device and turn around. The image, developed from low-energy X- or gamma rays, may show anything on the body; plastic explosives, plastic knives, guns and other contraband. Although the radiation is extremely low, some people protest even those levels. It is less than 1%, however, of the natural level we typically receive every day. Since the picture reveals the person's sex, some find it an invasion of privacy to have their body viewed by security personnel. The ACLU remarked that body scanning is an intrusive technology and passengers have the right to expect they will not be seen naked. The scanner maker, on the other hand, says the body scan is non-intrusive and far less objectionable than patting down the body.

While some people are offended by having their body image revealed, the screen also shows everything a person is carrying; metal, dynamite, C-4 explosives, ceramics, graphite fibers, plastics, packaged narcotics, bundled currency and even wooden objects. It is efficient at detecting dangerous devices, whether of

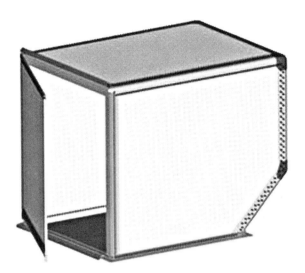

Explosion-proof cargo containers are reinforced to withstand bomb blast in belly of airplane. (Galaxy)

Appearance of the re-inforced cargo container after a bomb inside was detonated

composite, metal or organic material. Clearly, after September 11, modesty is one of our least concerns.

To have a truly safe airline system, with no threats to passenger safety, we must swallow our objections and accept new technologies for what they offer, rather than what they reveal about our bodies. "The goal must be," said Jane Garvey of the FAA, "100 percent screening of all passengers, baggage, and of airport and airline personnel."

Biometrics

The science of measuring distinctive human traits, such as fingerprints, DNA or photographs, is biometrics. It includes face recognition, hand geometry, iris (color portion of the eye) and scans of the retina. Each has advantages, but the common element is a unique identification that can be stored on passports, smart cards, in databases and other devices.

Face-recognition cameras compare passengers' biometrics against law-enforcement databases in real time---at the check-in counter. Before a passenger boards an airplane, he or she may be eliminated as a suspect. This one-stop identification greatly speeds security checks.

Smart Cards

German citizens have a computerized "smart" card that stores personal data for accessing that country's health care system. While a national identity card may not be adopted in the U.S., there are advocates of a voluntary program for frequent travelers who want to expedite security. Such passengers could have a fingerprint, iris scan, voice recognition or other data stored on the card for positive identification. Fingerprints are a good choice because they are accurate, fast, non-intrusive and cost-effective.

Chicago's O'Hare was the first airport to suggest upgrading to fingerprint recognition. Fitted to 1,100 access doors, a sensor would capture fingerprints of airport workers and digitize them on a smart card. Privacy is protected because the data cannot be reconstructed to reveal fingerprints and information is not stored in any other database. To open a door, an employee inserts the card, then places a finger on an optical sensor for permission to enter.

Body scanner, left, uses low-level X- or gamma-rays to show non-metal and metal objects.The amount of radiation is said to be less than 1 percent of that received by natural background levels, or well below national and international guidelines.

The scanner generates images shown below. Objects that may appear include; plastic explosives, plastic knifes, guns and other contraband. And possibly an intimate detail or two. (Photos courtesy of Rapiscan.)

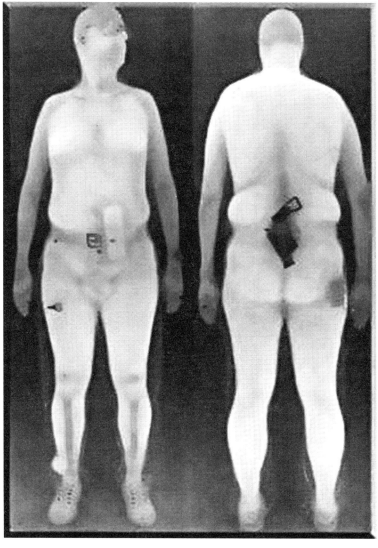

Similar systems have been suggested for pilots opening cockpit doors from outside.

Face Recognition

Some airports in Europe already use this technology. Police in Tampa, Florida pioneered face-recognition with dozens of street corner cameras in a popular nightclub district to check for criminals. Software breaks a person's face into a unique set of numbers called an "eigenface".

The algorithms (or rules) are based on Principle Component Analysis (PCA) developed at the Massachusetts Institute Technology. With an ordinary PC, the face of a person is compared to 1 million stored faces *per second*. Law enforcement databases may be integrated with face recognition, so no suspect will pass through an airport unchecked.

There are benefits to such surveillance, but privacy is worrisome to some people. The ACLU says face recognition breaches Fourth Amendment rights of protection against search and seizure, arguing that people should not automatically be included in an electronic lineup simply as a function of walking down the street. These concerns, however, are in regard to law enforcement and have not surfaced for airline security.

The case for face recognition in airports, however, relies on the fact that everyone is considered a potential terrorist simply by being a airline passenger. That's why your bags are scanned and you submit to security checks before being allowed to ride on an airplane. Face recognition is another step in the process of proving that people do not pose a threat.

Chapter 3

Air Marshals

The Air Marshal program began in 1968 to curb a rash of hijackings to Cuba. Originally called "sky marshals," and part of U.S. Customs, the program was extended in 1985 after a long and nasty hijacking that resulted in the death of a young American.

TWA flight 847 was hijacked out of Athens, Greece and diverted to Beirut, Lebanon, where more terrorists got on board. The airplane flew around the Middle East for two weeks, the hijackers demanding release of Shiite prisoners held by Israel. When the aircraft was seized on the ground, U.S. Navy diver Robert Stethem was murdered. The hijackers released the passengers, blew up the airplane and fled. As hijackings declined in the 1990s, the number of air marshals dwindled, leaving guards only on international flights.

Revived Program

After September 11, President Bush expanded the Air Marshal Program so U.S. flights would eventually have armed guards. The FAA added law enforcement officers from other agencies and recruited from among thousands of applicants. The age limit, 37 , was later amended to 40. Also added was a proviso that people with previous law enforcement experience may be over 40.

Transportation Secretary Norman Mineta queried the wisdom of the FAA's age limit, suggesting that displaced pilots might make perfect candidates so the age limit should be in the mid-forties. After all, he said, ex-pilot air marshals could also fly the plane in an emergency. There is a problem with this plan. A furlowed pilot hired as an air marshal will almost definitely resign if called back to work by his airline.

How They Operate

Air marshals are trained to use minimum force but it could become lethal. Applicants pass firearm, psychological and fitness tests. They train rigorously for fitness and firearm skills. Before every mission, they go through recurrent training and preparation.

The marshals train in Atlantic City, New Jersey for 14 weeks at outdoor shooting ranges, simulated aircraft cabins and two actual aircraft. There are outdoor ranges with moving targets and a 360-degree live-fire shoothouse simulating narrow- and wide-body airplanes. Targets are computer-controlled from a bullet-proof observation platform. An outdoor laser device judges shooting accuracy.

Air marshals also train in close-quarters countermeasures and personal defense with protective equipment and dummies. The New Jersey facility has an air traffic control tower, two retired airplanes (a B-727 and L-1011), classrooms, fitness center and operations. Other training centers around the country have not been disclosed because of security concerns.

Passenger Safeguards

A concern about air marshals is accidentally shooting innocent passengers or damaging the pressurized airplane. They are not only expert shots, but fire hollow-point, aluminum bullets that penetrate the body but disintegrate against hard surfaces. In a demonstration on the L-1011, air marshals, playing hijackers with knives, took flight attendants hostage and rushed the cockpit. The real air marshals drew weapons and shot the "hijackers" (with paint pellets). Innocent passengers were instructed to place their hands on their heads to assure they held no weapons.

The value of air marshals is well proven, but with thousands of daily flights there is no way they can be everywhere. Certain flights are at high risk, such as Washington DC, New York, New Jersey, Boston, Chicago, Los Angeles and San Francisco. They should be protected by air marshals, but daily flights from these cities are so numerous, not every one can be covered. Yet, there is a deterrent value, some say, because terrorists can't predict which flights are protected.

Help from Traveling Police

But let's say a terrorist hijacks a flight out of Raleigh-Durham, North Carolina. Are all these flights going to be covered by air marshals? The point is, terrorists will select flights less likely to have air marshals. Smaller airports, from Duluth, Minnesota to Long Beach, California, could very well suit hijackers' goal of wreaking terror.

To fill this gap, one solution is licensing state law enforcement officers to carry their firearms when they travel on aircraft. There is no doubt that armed protection on a flight deters terrorist attacks. It is only one measure, however, in an arsenal of improvements needed before the airline industry is truly safe.

Stray Bullets: Dangerous?

In my view, air marshals have a proven history of making airlines safe. There is risk of shooting an innocent passenger, but note that El Al operated three decades without shooting accidents. If you are ever a passenger where an air marshal goes into action, be sure to stay down, but keep your hands visible at all times. Putting your hands on the seat in front or on your head indicates to an air marshal that you are not a threat.

Bullet Holes

Assume that bullets are fired and the pressurized cabin is punctured. The holes would be so small that rapid, dangerous decompression is extremely unlikely. An opening the size of a cabin window, however, might create a problem. The pressurization system regulates a flow of air, tapped off the engines, which is air-conditioned and pumped into the cabin. Air then reaches outflow valves that regulate cabin pressure, under control of a computer that senses changes. If the cabin suffers a small puncture and pressure drops, the outflow valve closes just enough to compensate for the loss. You may hear the noise of air whistling out of the hole but the cabin structure should not be seriously affected.

There's plenty of redundancy in today's aircraft to meet this problem. If a hydraulic line (which affects flight control surfaces) ruptures and pressure is lost, this alone will not affect safety of flight. Similarly, if damaged avionics equipment overloads the electrical system, circuit breakers will trip and isolate the problem. All critical flight instruments are duplicated. The captain's and copilot's instruments and radios are independent. If a system on one side fails, the pilot transfers instruments from the good system. Even if all electrical systems fail, standby instruments continue to operate from the aircraft battery. Concern over bullets critically damaging the aircraft are unfounded.

Air marshals are well-versed in how terrorists think and trained in counter-strategies. It is extremely unlikely that an air marshal will have his or her gun taken away, but if this happens there would be a problem. But the chances are insignificant compared to the consequences of not responding to the crisis.

Limiting the age of air marshals to the early 40's is also a mistake. If a terrorist looks around at the passengers, he would see people under 40, physically fit, bearing a confident attitude and seated on an aisle. Any undercover operation, therefore, should make the agent undetectable. If terrorists narrow the list of passengers to possible air marshals, that knowledge may cause them to attack these suspects first.

Chapter 4

Passenger Self-Defense

On United Flight 93 four male passengers voted to tackle terrorists who had taken over the airplane. In calls to loved ones via cell phone, they reported that several flight attendants and passengers had been stabbed. Calling himself the "captain," one terrorist ordered everyone to stay quiet and remain seated while the airplane returned to the airport. A second hijacker pointed to a "bomb" strapped to his body (another lie).

Exactly what happened in the cabin is not certain, but officials are sure passengers devised a plan to thwart the terrorists. An FBI official later said, "I can confirm that passengers engaged in a fight for their lives...and most likely saved the lives of unknown individuals on the ground."

After a series of incidents following September 11, the new reality was suddenly clear. Everyday citizens can not only act in concert to overpower terrorists---they *must*, or they may not survive. The action on flight 93 was heroic, but it began over an hour after the airplane was taken over. Now we know that a response to terrorists in the cabin must be swift, forceful and cooperative. It is hardly the time to obey tyrants' orders or cower in fear.

Airline pilots supported the idea. On a United flight, the captain urged passengers to take whatever objects in their possession ---shoes, books, glasses, briefcases---and throw it at the *heads* of anyone who attempted to commandeer the airplane. He shouted a phrase from the Constitution; "We the people" to bolster passenger confidence. "We will not be defeated," he declared, as everyone in the cabin applauded, saying they now felt in control.

The wisdom is simple; if every person on board becomes a brother or sister in arms, terrorists wouldn't stand a chance. A massive reaction can blunt the assailant's powerful tools of surprise, shock and intimidation.

Passengers Respond

In the rash of incidents following September 11, passengers echoed the idea:

"You can't just sit there anymore," said Tony Lanier, a former high school linebacker who flies four times a week. "If someone rushes the cockpit...I'd do anything to stop it."

"It's a sorry person who would sit still during a hijacking now," said Donald Avery, an auto mechanic.

Gordon Langford, on a trip to Phoenix, vowed "to do what it takes or go down fighting."

The Airline Pilots Association commented; "Security is as much the passengers' business as it is the flight crews'."

Flight attendants pleaded for self-defense training. Their national association pushed vigorously in Washington for guidelines on what they could do in the cabin.

A bizarre affirmation of this idea happened five months after September 11. A passenger kicked a hole in the bottom of the cockpit door on a flight between Miami and Argentina, and thrust his head through the opening. (The door had only an iron bar across it.) The pilot immediately called on the P.A. for help. Several passengers leaped on the man on the cabin side and pinned him down. Inside the cockpit, the co-pilot struck the man with the side of a crash axe. A tragedy averted, passengers strapped the man with belts.

This incident happened after massive security measures were

Hurl objects at the assailants. Use almost anything at hand; a bag, laptop, books, seat cushions , shoes, etc. The impact can be impressive
if done by a large group. One flight attendant
recommends "aiming at the head". It's several
hundred passengers against few individuals.

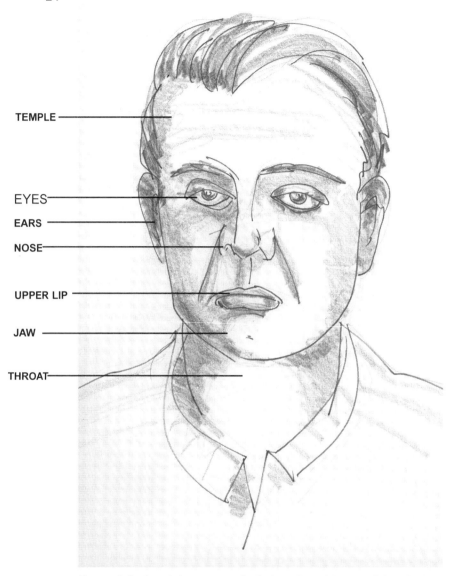

TEMPLE

EYES

EARS

NOSE

UPPER LIP

JAW

THROAT

Parts of the head that are particularly vulnerable to striking. Poke a finger or sharp object like a ball-point pen into the assailant's eye. This is not an open-handed maneuver; keep it to one finger or a sharp object. A thumb is an excellent digit for this defense because it is robust and offers a better angle for striking an opponent who is beside or slightly behind you. Finger jabs, clawing, stabbing and hooked finger, sometimes referred to as the "chicken beak," are also effective. The assailant may sustain injuries that are painful and debilitating.

in place. It's becoming clear that no matter how sophisticated the airport security or how well cockpit doors are fortified, passengers are the front-line protection against disaster. Let's consider the role of a passenger when the cabin is suddenly threatened.

Psych'ing Up

After the Civil War, Yankee soldiers told fearsome stories of the "rebel yell." One veteran described how Confederate soldiers screamed with such ferocity while attacking, it sent a "corkscrew sensation up one's spine." At a Civil War reunion, a 93-year-old Confederate veteran let loose the fabled cry. It startled Union veterans, catapulting them back to the battlefield. When the old man was asked to repeat the performance, he hesitated, saying he could do it only at a dead run in full charge against the enemy.

For centuries soldiers have struck fear in the enemy, while raising their own courage, with their voices. You may have done it, while riding a roller coaster screaming as you plunged down. Maybe you laughed or grunted, but whatever the sound, you were releasing fear and bolstering courage. Adrenaline flows and energy increases in the face of danger. These mechanisms also unsettle your adversary.

In Karate, *Kiai* is a means of startling one's opponent. It's not a true yell because the sound is not drawn out. It's rapid exhaling from the lungs, usually vocalized with 'EEE' or 'HEE'. It does three things:

Expelling air contracts your stomach muscles. Try it and note the effect. If an opponent strikes, you are better able to withstand the blow. The wind won't be knocked out of you.

A loud Kiai is startling, causing momentary loss of focus by your opponent. Now you have a window of opportunity to strike. The rush of adrenaline from your Kiai bolsters your resolve and powers an aggressive attack. In other words, it psychs you up.

Your adversary knows this, too. I'm reasonably certain that on September 11 loud commands were shouted at passengers and crew. By surprising a group of untrained civilians, it produced the desired reaction; subservience. That's why you need to know how it works.

Another truism of combat is: the best defense is attack. What's more, you attack when the assailant feels most powerful! Remember Newton's Law of Motion; "Every action has an equal and opposite reaction." If your attacker yells, instead of cowering, attack with a loud Kiai. This should surprise your assailant, who may become momentarily disoriented. It works to your advantage, helping you strike with a coordinated, aggressive defense.

Pile On

Gang-rush the assailants. Use seat cushions as shields against knives. With fist, palm or elbow, strike at the man's vulnerable areas, as shown in illustrations. Nose strikes cause intense pain. There are many nerve endings under the top lip, another target. Strike between the eyes at the top of the nose. Many people think that this will push a bone into the brain and cause instantaneous death, but it's untrue. Damage is from shock transferred to the brain. Exceptionally strong blows can cause unconsciousness.

To make a fist, curl fingers tightly so they touch the bottom part of your fingers. It takes practice to curl tightly, so try it several times. Secondly, fold in your thumb so it sits against your curled fingers. As a general rule, in hand strikes the thumb curls or folds inward toward the palm of your hand to prevent it from snagging and sustaining injury during the blow.

Striking the man's temple with a closed fist may stun him. Most people believe the skull is thinner in this area, but this is not true---it is only flatter. The force of a strong blow to the temple causes disorientation or unconsciousness due to shock transfer to the brain.

Striking the throat with the tips of four fingers can be devastating. You can also use the side of an open hand in a classic Karate chop. Even a semi-delivered blow can cause the assailant to cough and wheeze. Fingers pushed into the sensitive, hollow V-point at the base of the throat can cause great pain and likely result in releasing a hold.

The swing of an elbow can develop substantial force. When striking with your elbow (left arm ,for example), begin by crossing your arms across your body. Make sure the fists of both hands are clenched to ensure that muscles in your arms are flexed. Simultaneously bring your left arm across your body striking your opponent while moving your right arm in the opposite direction. This will create more power in your strike.

Scratching into the flesh as strongly as possible can cause pain, and the release of the assailant's grip.

Target areas for body strikes are knees, groin, thighs, feet, kidneys, solar plexus, spine, neck, shoulder, hands and fingers. With the inside or outside side of the foot, kick to the side and downward along the side of the assailant's knee. This can incapacitate the attacker and cause debilitating pain. Even kicking the back of his knee may cause him to crumple to the floor.

Kicks

Kicks are effective in bringing down an assailant. One is a cross kick, where you lift your knee high and bring it down across the front of your body against the knee of your opponent. In a thrust kick, bring your knee up across your body and bring it down in an outward motion against your assailant's knee. Third, lift your knee and swing it in a roundhouse kick to the side of your attacker's knee.

The groin can be struck with the foot, knee or hand. One defensive move that may bring immediate incapacitation is to grab the man's genitals, squeeze and not let go. If there's enough room, a good kick in this area is a groin kick. Lift the knee high and kick out with the lower part of her leg, using the knee as a fulcrum.

The groin kick starts by lifting your leg high then delivering the blow using the knee as a fulcrum. Whether the attacker is struck by the instep of your foot or shinbone will not matter---both are effective in disabling an attacker.

Using a knee, strike at the outer side of the man's thigh. This is less effective than the knee or groin, but a good strike causes great pain and makes it difficult to remain standing. The upper inside of the thigh, halfway to the knee has a large number of nerves under the skin, which makes it an effective strike area. Even

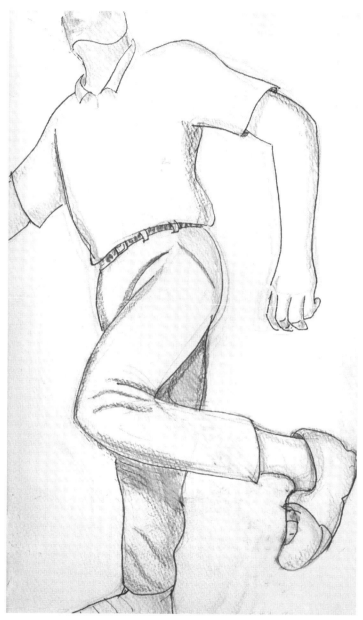

Kicks can deliver powerful blows. Lift the knee high and swing your foot to attacker's knee. Also, scrape your feet along the shin. Strike other parts, too.

Striking with the heel of the palm just below the ear can cause sufficient pain for the assailant to release a hold. If delivered to the jaw with full force, the teeth may break or he may bite down on his tongue, causing severe bleeding.

Throat

Two glands just beneath the chin on either side of the esophagus, cause intense pain when squeezed. If necessary, grab the assailant by the throat and squeeze these glands. The intruder may be incapacitated under this grip.

Collar Bone

The collar bone (between the shoulder and the neck) is close to the skin and easily broken using strong techniques such as a hammer blow, open hand or elbow strike. A broken collar bone will cause intense pain and restrict the assailant's use of his arm and shoulder.

Hand Twist

Grab the assailant's hand and twist towards the thumb (the unnatural direction). It's effective in forcing him to release his grip. The trick is to twist the wrist in the opposite direction in which it normally moves.

If you can grab a finger and pull it back strongly, this can force him to release his grip. It reduces his capacity to use the hand in further attacks. Another technique to force the release of a grip is to scratch into flesh with all your might. This causes an intense stinging pain. The injury, though, is not debilitating and the technique could enrage him further. He will almost certainly turn his aggressive attention to the person who scratched him. So be prepared: once his grip is released do not hesitate to use more damaging strikes.

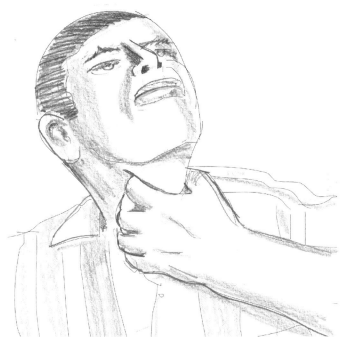

Pressure in the neck area is effective because it's not protected by strong muscles. It can be used to walk the assailant
backwards (with the help of fellow passengers). Avoid pro-
longed choke hold to prevent permanent injury.

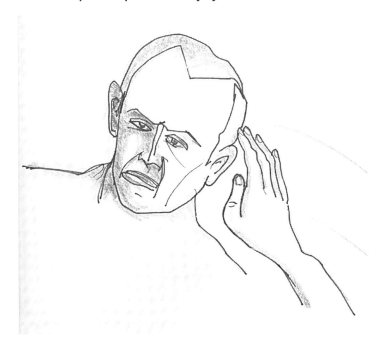

A cupped hand forcefully struck over an ear can
cause disorientation.

Restraining the Assailant

Passengers should grab the disabled attacker from behind in a choke hold. Walking backwards while strongly locking an arm around the attacker's throat, the assailant is unable to retaliate. The man may strike out with his legs at anyone who attempts to restrain his legs. Options at this point are limited by crewmembers' and passengers' strength and willingness to assist in restraining the man. It is imperative that he be totally prevented from damaging the cabin.

Note: The choke hold can be dangerous and it is your decision to use it as a restraint technique. If done correctly, no permanent harm is done, but not if the person's trachea is closed off. However, in a life-threatening situation, few methods are better at incapacitating an assailant. In 10 to 20 seconds, the man loses consciousness. If this happens, the person applying pressure to the throat needs to make a critical decision on whether to continue applying or relax pressure and hope the assailant is not feigning unconsciousness. Be aware that if the assailant passes out, he may regain consciousness in 20 to 30 seconds after pressure is released. This gives only small window of opportunity for your next phase.

It is critical that the man's feet be restrained before or immediately after relaxing pressure on the neck---even by several burly passengers sitting on them. Take a moment to compare the muscles of your arm with those in your leg. Besides larger size there is extra leverage in lower limbs because of greater length. A kick delivers far more destructive force than a punch. Crew members and passengers, therefore, will have to cooperate and tie the man's feet as soon as possible. Use seat belt extensions if nothing else is available. Handcuff straps are ideal, but duct tape can also bind the man's hands and feet. Tape his limbs to a passenger seat so he is completely immobilized.

Most of the fight, we expect by now, is knocked out of the attacker. But don't hesitate to strike him, if necessary, in any target area as often as needed. Take whatever action to tie the man's hands behind his back. Remember, even tied hands can be used in

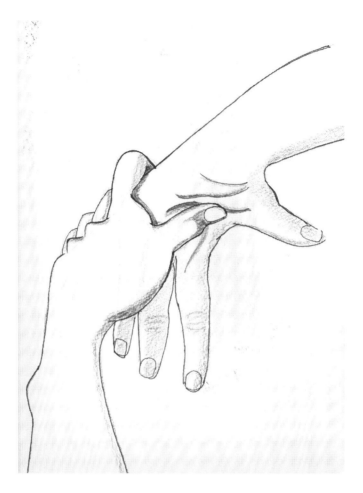

Twisting hand in unnatural direction may loosen its grip

Pulling back one finger may help release a grip.

front of the man's body. Before landing, put the man in a passenger seat, if possible, but if he is too heavy or resists, leave him in a prone position on the cabin floor. Guard him with strong men until police take him into custody. It may be necessary to prevent angry passengers from continuing to strike after the assailant has been restrained.

Cabin Scenario

Let's consider how these events might play out. The flight has been uneventful since takeoff. As the airplane approaches cruise altitude, flight attendants Val and Jen are in the forward cabin handing out headsets and beginning beverage service. Without attracting much attention, four men in different sections stand and casually move toward the front of the cabin. Val sees two of them and alarm bells sound inside her head. She and the other flight attendants had briefed before takeoff on what to do if this situation arose, but she momentarily freezes in horror; both men are trying to conceal a weapon in their hands. As their eyes meet, one terrorist realizes his cover is blown. He yells and each man rushes toward Val and Jen. In the rear galley, Jack is preparing meals.

There is no time for Val to give covert messages to Jan or any other crew member. She reverts to training received in her company's anti-terrorist program. Although scared out of her wits, she yells two words at the top of her lungs;

"Help!...Hijack!"

Passengers were aware of something amiss, but on those two shouts many stand and confront the hijackers. Knife-wielding terrorists slash viciously. Nearby passengers, splashed with blood, recoil in horror. One hijacker reaches Val, grabs her and holds the knife to her throat. He screams, "Stay back or I will kill her!" Passengers shrink from the hijackers, who move toward the front galley.

In the rear galley Jack hears Val's warning and calls the cockpit. He tells the pilots that armed hijackers are attacking flight attendants and passengers in the cabin. The pilots notify Air Traffic Control and begin an emergency descent. The copilot flicks a control and rapidly depressurizes the cabin. The captain banks the

Head butt to soft tissues of the face can help subdue the assailant.

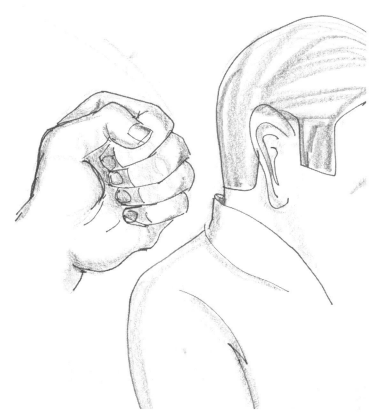

The collar bone is a vulnerable target. Located between the neck and shoulder it is close to the skin and easily injured, limiting motion of the arm and shoulder. Strike with a sharp blow of your fist, arm or elbow.

wings into a steep roll and forces the nose down. He hopes the extreme maneuvers and loss of cabin pressure will physically upset the hijackers in the cabin.

Jack in the rear grabs a fire extinguisher and tosses unopened cans of soda to passengers in the rear section. Every person on board is disoriented, reeling from the violent flight maneuvers, but many are armed with projectiles. Jack instructs them to overpower the hijackers.

Up forward, the hijackers stagger around the rolling and pitching cabin. The assailant with a knife to Val's throat maintains his grip as they both ricochet from side to side. Val waits until she feels the blade move slightly away from her neck. She puts both arms in front of her, grabs the hijacker's forearm and pushes with all her strength. She rapidly doubles over, pushing her backside into the hijacker's body. Her defensive move succeeds and she slides beneath the blade to the floor, but suffers a cut to the cheek. Before the hijacker regains composure, a heavy barrage of soda cans, shoes and handbags assault the terrorists' heads. As they raise arms to protect their faces, the passengers press the attack. Each person yells and strikes with fists and objects. Jack leaps up and sprays the fire extinguisher in the face of Val's attacker. Val ducks the blade and screams, punching him in his genitals with every ounce of strength she can muster. He crumples and Jack bangs the fire extinguisher to the base of his skull.

In short order, all hijackers are disarmed and beaten into submission. Several are unconscious, but Val and the other flight attendants bind their hands and feet. Jack informs the pilots the hijackers have been overcome---and the captain resumes normal flight. After landing, local authorities arrest the terrorists while crew members and passengers embrace in victory. Luckily, only three passengers received gashes; none, however, life-threatening.

These scenarios suggest how situations might play out with a predetermined strategy involving all crew members. Keep in mind that even the best plans will not account for every possibility. Each person must use his or her initiative to deal with unique circumstances. Routine training, practice and knowledge of defense tactics, however, makes improvisation much easier, as well as quick cooperation from passengers.

Anticipate

Some lessons learned are: remain alert, watch an argumentative passenger's eyes, hands, stance and other body language for signs of aggression. Body language is more reflective of a person's mood, attitude and possible misbehavior than the spoken word. Look for nervousness, furtive glances between passengers and other suspicious behavior. Do not wait until the doors lock and the airplane pushes back from the gate. Act immediately and tell authorities. Innocent passengers will not object to extra scrutiny and most will appreciate that security is the highest priority. We've summarized the basic rules on the next page, but most important is:

**At the first sign of trouble in the cabin,
shout for help. Quickly form a support
group and take action.**

BASIC RULES

1. Look around the cabin. Observe suspicious or nervous behavior. This includes a passenger who wants to talk to the pilots.

2. Check your seat-neighbors for possible allies.

3. If suspicious behavior becomes an obvious, full-blown threat;

   SHOUT AT THE TOP OF YOUR LUNGS---"*HELP-HELP-HELP*"

   Quickly inform the whole cabin to form a group.

4. Do not obey terrorist orders to herd to the back of the airplane or get on the floor.

5. Do not be intimidated by bomb threats or weapons. You're not alone.

6. Shout for everyone to throw objects at the assailants' heads ---bags, laptops, trays, etc. Keep up a steady barrage.

7. Rapidly gang-rush the assailants as a group--- crush them to the floor, restrain them. Use the protective and defensive tactics described in this chapter.

TO SUM UP

   • Be alert to warning signs
   • Summon a group quickly (Scream like a banshee.)
   • Don't hesitate. Move swiftly, together.
   • Gang-rush the assailants, crush them to the floor.
   • Use protective measures in this chapter.
   • Exploit the overwhelming power of angry
     neighbors determined to fight back.

Chapter 5

Air Rage

Even before September 11, incidents of air rage were mounting. Whether caused by alcohol, drugs, a deranged mentality or psychological problems, the self-defense techniques are much the same as described for terrorism. Let's consider several scenarios based on actual events. Since cockpits are now difficult to infiltrate and pilots duty-bound not to leave their positions under any circumstances, flight attendants are on their own.

Mayhem Aloft

The first case is an enraged, large-framed male who demands to be taken to the cockpit. Our MD-80 is almost at cruise altitude when a passenger, who has been grumbling to flight attendants and nearby travelers, gets out of his seat and walks toward the forward cabin. He takes off his jacket, loosens his tie and tears at his shirt sleeves as if they are irritating his skin. As he nears the flight attendant at the rear of a service cart, he yells, "Get out of my way! I want to see the captain!"

The flight attendant (let's call her "Anne") notices the man's face is red, he's perspiring, his eyes filled with anger. She says over her shoulder to her co-worker at the forward end of the cart, "Jan, will you see if we have any Evian in the forward galley please." (This is a code prearranged by the flight crew to warn of such an event.)

The other flight attendant quickly goes to the forward galley and calls all stations on the interphone. She relates the situation to the pilots, who immediately notify the ground they have a problem passenger and to standby. The pilots rehearse their pre-briefed actions in case the man invades the cockpit. Other flight attendants stand by to help but do not approach for fear of irritating the enraged passenger. Jan talks to several male passengers near the forward galley and asks them to jump to her assistance if the passenger rushes toward the cockpit.

Anne tries to calm the man and escort him to the rear of the cabin---the furthest distance from the cockpit. She placates him in a soothing voice and promises to attend his needs. Suddenly, he pushes her violently. She falls in the aisle and strikes her head on an arm rest. She lies there stunned as the man steps over her and rushes forward. A male passenger stands up and tries to intercede but is pushed aside.

Jan sees the man coming forward and yells "Help" at the top of her lungs.

Three male passengers leap up and surround her. The man attempts to break through, striking one person in the face and pushing Jan aside. The two other passengers leap on the man's back but his momentum and size keep him upright.

Jan is shaken but regains her stability. She raises a foot and smashes it down sideways against the man's knee. He screams in pain and falls to the floor. The two passengers pummel him into submission. Jan rushes to the forward galley for restraining devices and secures the man's feet and legs.

Helped by male passengers, Jan and other flight attendants put the assailant in a seat and strap his arms and legs to the chair. Jan asks passengers to rearrange their seating so those assisting can sit near the subdued man. They monitor his status and alert each other if further restraint is necessary.

Anne appears fine but will need medical treatment for a large bump on the head. When she rises and walks to her seat, passengers cheer her valor. Jan informs the captain the situation is under control and the man is fully restrained and monitored by male passengers. The captain informs the ground of the situation and asks federal authorities to meet the airplane. The incident is ended.

Conflicting Reports

Working in the cabin, flight attendants bear the brunt of passenger abuse and assault. According to the Association of Flight Attendants (AFL-CIO), an estimated 4,000 air rage incidents occur each year, and most are not reported. Airlines have the option of reporting incidents to the FAA, but most do not. One major US airline's internal reports of air rage incidents for 1999 total 454, while the FAA's records show only 310 incidents reported industry-wide for the same period.

Air rage is a felony with a possible 20-year jail sentence, plus criminal and civil penalties ranging to $25,000. Nevertheless, violent passengers continue to assault flight crew members. One reason may be that in 18 months between January 2000 and June 2001 only 18 civil fines were imposed on air rage perpetrators and only one had been collected. Another problem in prosecuting abusive passengers is the gray area of jurisdiction, particularly when incidents occur on international flights.

What Makes a Wacko?

NASA compiled a database of 2,600 incidents to shed light on air rage. Here's what it found:
- 43% involved alcohol.
- 51% involved unlawful interference with crew members.
- 24% resulted in physical assaults on crew members.
- 22% caused pilots to leave the cockpit to deal with the situation.
- 41% were a significant distraction to pilots.
- 10% involved more than one irate passenger.

The forces driving air rage fit into five categories:
- Alcohol
- Drugs
- No smoking limitations.
- Prohibited use of electronic devices.
- Bomb or hijack threats.

Ancillary causes of obnoxious or violent behavior:
- Number of travelers in airport.
- Overcrowded flights.

- Cramped seating.
- Excessive carryon baggage.
- Frequent delays and cancellations.
- Conflicts over policies, such as passenger bumping.
- Differences between reality and airline advertisements

Flight attendants are not trained in negotiation, psychology or self defense. Nevertheless, they are abused psychologically and physically almost daily, given little respect for their professionalism, and generally treated as punching bags for passengers venting frustration. Seemingly normal passengers defecate and urinate in the cabin, attempt to open emergency exits, bust through cockpit doors, scratch, bite, spit, slap, punch...you name it!

Let's take a closer look at actual incidents over the years to detect any common elements. This exercise also highlights defenses that work and those that won't.

Mental Cases Need Escorts

On a flight from Los Angeles to Chicago a mentally deranged man stormed the cockpit. The man's father had passed a note to flight attendants saying his son was unstable and might become violent. It took three seconds for the 6-ft 2-in, 180-pound man to blast through the cockpit door as if it were tissue paper. Six men were needed to restrain him while plastic cuffs and eight seat belt extensions restrained his movement. One problem was that buckles on the seat belt extensions kept popping open while the man "writhed on the floor like a possessed demon." The flight landed safely, but the passenger had to be physically restrained by five men during the landing, despite being sedated.

A potentially violent passenger should not be allowed to travel without an escort, but our job is to learn from this experience. Two problems emerge: the need for cockpit bulkhead and door reinforcement is obvious, as well as restraining devices in the cabin within easy reach of flight attendants.

If an airline carries plastic cuffs, they are usually located in the cockpit. One easy solution for flight attendants is a roll or two of duct tape in the cabin. Duct tape has myriad uses and a new one might include binding the hands and feet of violent passengers.

Cockpit modifications are underway to fortify bulkheads, door jambs, latches, hinges and doors against intrusion. Ultimately, cockpits will be impervious to attack and pilots will be protected. Flight attendants, though, stand alone in the cabin, unprotected. Even if airlines begin training in negotiation skills, such methods would fall short in dealing with mentally unstable passengers. Whether we like it or not, what needs to be taught to every flight attendant is the art of self defense.

Flight attendants were quick to ask for, and receive, passenger assistance in the case above. Since September 11, 2001, passengers are far more inclined to come to the rescue and, in my opinion, that is a good thing. It is imperative in dealing with an enraged passenger that many participants be recruited.

Double Trouble

A flight attendant was slapped in the face and crew members assaulted by twin sisters on flight from San Francisco to Shanghai, China. The sisters were denied alcohol earlier, after becoming boisterous. One sister was so enraged she attempted to kick down a lavatory door. When a female flight attendant told her to calm down, the passenger struck her in the face. When other flight attendants came to the rescue, the two sisters were moved to a section of the cabin with few passengers. Attempts to calm them failed. Because of the sisters' vile behavior, the captain diverted to Anchorage, Alaska and had them off-loaded.

The flight attendants acted with superb control, helped by group action. The fact that the women were not restrained was probably more due to their being women than anything else. The pilot, however, should not have come into the cabin to confront the situation. Even if he were off duty, his prime responsibility is to rest so he could relieve the other pilots later in the flight. If he had been injured, the operating pilots would be compelled to continue the flight without rest. Obviously, this jeopardizes the operation of the airplane.

No Justice

A deranged 27-year-old man stormed into the cockpit of a Boeing 747-400 enroute from London to Nairobi and tried to seize control. Unbelievably, despite such assaults on the cockpit, the airline's policy was to keep the cockpit door unlocked during cruise. In the scuffle that followed, the autopilot disconnected and the aircraft went into a violent dive. It injured several passengers and broke the ankle of a flight attendant. The captain apologized for having to disable his attacker by "poking him in the eye".

The aircraft landed safely in Nairobi, where the young man was placed in a psychiatric hospital. Incredibly, a doctor diagnosed him as suffering severe paranoia when he stormed the cockpit, probably triggered, he said, by extreme *exam* stress. Under these circumstances, the local attorney general decided not to charge the young man with a criminal offense. Not much solace for passengers and crew scared witless.

Apart from the lack of common sense in keeping the cockpit door unlocked, the captain performed a perfect assailant-disabling technique: a poke in the eye. Whether one uses a finger, a pen or other object, a poke in the eye disorients and momentarily disables an attacker while reinforcements are mustered. It is not a dirty tactic, but a sound defensive move against an attacker who can cause your death.

Another point; there must have been warning signs missed by cabin crew and passengers. It easy to play armchair quarterback after the event, but this man must have been agitated, exhibiting distress before storming the flight deck. That must have been apparent to people in his vicinity. He may have had angry words with a flight attendant before he lost control. In other words, opportunities were missed where defenses could have been set in place before the event. Flight attendants could have asked male passengers seated around the man to watch his behavior. A flight attendant could have been stationed near the cockpit door.

The lessons of this case are watch for threats, think about methods of restraint and set defenses in place--anything to help flight attendants thwart violent behavior.

Authorities must come down hard on violent passengers. In this case, the young man was virtually excused from threatening everyone's life. Exam stress? I don't think so.

Stiff fines and jail terms apply to air rage felons in the U.S., but the full extent of the law is rarely applied. In other jurisdictions, arbitrary punishment hardly seems fair or just. To impress the public that interference with the operation of airplanes will bring severe penalties, it must be enforced by all nations.

Lethal Attack

In another serious incident, a 19-year-old assailant died while being restrained by passengers on a flight from Las Vegas to Salt Lake City. The young man kicked a hole in the cockpit door, tried to open an emergency hatch and punched several male passengers who tried to restrain him. There were allegations that passengers overreacted and continued to beat a man who was already subdued. A U.S. Attorney decided not to press charges against passengers who, he claimed, acted in self defense.

This case set a legal precedent that may protect passengers and crew from criminal prosecution if an assailant dies after being subdued.

Captain's Assault

A drunken man broke into the cockpit of a charter flight from Berlin to the Canary Islands and began to punch, kick and choke the 59-year-old captain. After a plea of help from the copilot, burly passengers subdued the assailant and removed him from the cockpit.

The details of this case are sketchy, but one presumes the copilot busied himself with flying the airplane. Such an attack, if not discussed before flight, would come as a shock. It would be difficult to react other than to fend off blows. The critical point in this case is the need for a predetermined defense against cockpit intrusion. If a person anticipates an attack, which I advocate all pilots and flight attendants do on every flight, he or she is prepared mentally to fight the attacker. The difference between defense and fighting is that one is only fending off blows, while the other is actively delivering strikes to disorient and incapacitate an assailant.

Axe Incident

A 6-foot-2-inch, 250-pound passenger broke into the cockpit and attacked the pilots while enroute from Puerto Vallarta, Mexico to San Francisco. The man lunged at the controls and screamed, "I'm going to kill you!" The copilot, forewarned of the attack, armed himself with the crash ax. In the melee, the captain called frantically over the P.A. for passenger help. The assailant was restrained, but not before the copilot received a nasty gash on his hand. Luckily, the assailant did not gain full use of the ax, or we might have witnessed another tragedy.

Every cockpit has a crash axe for pilots to break their way out in an emergency. This case is particularly important because a weapon intended for the assailant was used against the copilot. What the copilot intended was appropriate, but keep in mind that this occurred before September 11, 2001. The copilot probably intended to scare, more than injure, the assailant. Irrational people, especially large, enraged men, do not scare easily.

While an axe may be a good weapon against an assailant who breaks into the cockpit, few individuals can strike a lethal blow without hesitation. All it takes is a millisecond for an assailant to take the weapon from you. Instead of the hunter, you become the hunted.

A better response would be for the pilots to quickly revised the defense of their cockpit and loosen their seat belts for ease of movement. When the man bursts through the cockpit door, the copilot could begin his attack, hitting the assailant as often and as hard as he can while the captain maintains control of the aircraft and calls for passenger help.

Another tactic is for one pilot to initiate a steep nose-down maneuver or steep bank to throw the intruder off balance.

This perpetrator had shown significant distress before attacking the flight deck---muttering threats and shredding clothing as he wandered up the aisle toward the cockpit. This was the time to redirect the man to another area to discuss his problems or enlist other passengers to prevent his actions.

Welcome No More

An enraged male passenger aboard a flight from Calgary to Halifax, Canada walked into the cockpit and attempted to assault the pilots. He was restrained in time and removed by passengers and flight attendants. The airline policy at that time was to keep the cockpit door unlocked except during takeoff and landing

The unlocked cockpit door was a mistake, given the number of passenger assaults on pilots. It seems apparent that airlines did not swap such information among themselves ---until September 11, when the industry became aware that cock pit doors must be locked and fortified.

Emergency Door

An inebriated passenger attempted to break into the cockpit of a flight from Los Angeles to Tokyo. He was foiled by several passengers and male flight attendants. Not happy at being thwarted in his original mission, the deranged man shouted, "Tonight, everybody will die!' He then tried to open an emergency exit door.

Once restrained from assaulting the cockpit, the passenger should not have been left unguarded in the cabin. This situation called for repositioning him in a seat and monitoring by volunteers---preferably large men. Plastic cuffs or other restraints were needed to prevent more harm.

Bloody Murder

In the most serious attack before September 11, 2001, a Boeing 747-400 captain was killed by an assailant who took over controls of the airplane and flew within 1,000 feet of the ground. Serious breaches of security enabled the assailant to smuggle an 8-inch knife on board. After takeoff, he pulled the knife, held it to a flight attendant's throat and made her unlock the cockpit door. He ordered the copilot to leave. The assailant instructed the captain to land at a U.S. naval base west of Tokyo. When the captain refused, the assailant stabbed him in the neck. With the deranged murderer now at the controls, the aircraft dropped within 1,000 feet of striking the terrain before the copilot and an off-duty pilot regained control. The motive for this premeditated crime? The man had grown bored with flight simulator computer games and wanted to experience the real thing.

Anti-hijack training for flight crew members is based on thirty-year-old data. Conventional wisdom says that if hijacker demands are met, a peaceful solution can be negotiated. This case, though, emphasizes that under no circumstances should a pilot leave the cockpit to assist flight attendants. This sounds cruel, given that a flight attendant might lose his or her life unless pilots comply and open cockpit doors. But the sad truth is that once inside the cockpit, everyone's life is at stake.

I am sure the flight attendant attacked in this case felt she had no other option than to open the cockpit door. When a knife is held at the throat, it is almost impossible to extricate yourself without serious injury. If this situation happens again, other flight attendants and passengers must leap to the victim's defense and attack the assailant enmasse. When an assailant is armed, he or she must be disarmed, and the best time is when the assailant feels most powerful---when he or she least expects resistance.

Cut Him Off

On a flight from Atlanta to Manchester, a passenger who had been denied alcohol assaulted flight attendants and attempted to enter the cockpit. He was restrained and the flight diverted to Bangor, Maine, where he was placed under arrest.

Alcohol is the cause in many incidents. And there is discussion on whether alcohol should be banned altogether on flights. Serving alcohol is a carry over from an age when air travel was a luxury that few people could afford. In my opinion (and I like to have the occasional beer) alcohol is a problem, so let's remove it once and for all. Unless the Department of Transportation acts on advice from Congress and bans alcohol from commercial flights, airlines are unlikely to take the initiative. It is as a worldwide phenomenon that should be deliberated by the International Air Transport Association and government regulatory authorities.

Difficult Listening

An abusive passenger broke into the cockpit of a flight while the pilots were attempting to land at Copenhagen, Denmark. The man shouted so loudly the pilots had trouble hearing instructions from Air Traffic Control. He was arrested after the aircraft landed.

Again, alcohol was the factor. The pilots probably just wanted to get the airplane on the ground and not aggravate the situation by striking the assailant, but the distraction was extremely dangerous. Loud noise is a bad enough, but abuse shouted in the ear arouses fear for one's safety. Flight attendants should have enlisted passenger assistance and wrestled the man back into the cabin.

In situations where the phase of flight puts a heavy workload on pilots (especially approach and landing), a violent passenger cannot be ignored. Rather than a calming effect, acquiescing to enraged people empowers them. While communication skills may soothe the riled, some situations demand an immediate response to remove the threat. In other words, action speaks louder than words.

Say You're Sorry

A passenger threatened a flight attendant, then began beating on the cockpit door with his fists. The passenger later claimed that a pilot had provoked him. (Anyone else hear the *Outer Limits* theme?)

Maybe a breakdown in communication aggravated this man. Perhaps sophisticated communication may have defused his problem. The real point is, the situation should never be allowed to deteriorate to where the man becomes so enraged his only response is to beat on the cockpit door. If apologies and negotiation fail, a passenger banging on the cockpit door must be stopped.

Knock Down, Drag Out

A 200-pound male passenger was restrained after trying to breakdown the cockpit door of a flight from Los Angeles to Baltimore. A female flight attendant, who tried to block the assailant's entry into the cockpit, sustained serious injuries after he threw her over several rows of seats.

This unlucky flight attendant joined the ranks of many who suffer serious injuries from passenger assaults. It is unfortunate that others in the cabin did not come to her assistance before she was attacked.

Knock Knock

A liquor-soused passenger entered the cockpit of a flight on its approach to Bangkok, Thailand. Passengers and crew removed him before he could do harm. Until this time, it had been airline policy to keep the cockpit door unlocked during cruise so flight attendants would not be "inconvenienced" when gaining entry.

Leaving the cockpit door unlocked has never been a good idea, as proven by numerous invasions and walk-ins. In my experience, I've had a drunk walk into the cockpit of a Boeing 727, thinking it was entry to the bathroom. Even when I convinced him of the error, he thought it was a good time to enlighten me on problems of the airline industry. Luckily, our lead flight attendant had good people skills and escorted the man back to the cabin before the situation deteriorated. Even after suffering several similar incidents, the airline still maintained an unlocked cockpit door policy.

Panic

A woman suffering from a panic attack, kicked open the cockpit door of a flight from Iowa to Minneapolis-St. Paul. Although she was quickly restrained by a cabin crew member and passenger, the pilots returned to the airport. Their ability to concentrate was disrupted.

Panic attack and depression are often treated with medication. Approximately 17 million Americans have been treated with Prozac alone and the drug has been proven effective over the last ten years. Yet, medication is only effective if taken in the correct dosage. In the case of Prozac, the drug's benefits may not become apparent for one to four weeks after starting, and success may take 6 to 12 months of monitoring. The point is, many people are on medication to control aberrant behavior and not all are taking the correct dosage.

This case shows that assailants are sometimes women. In another incident, a 69-year-old woman rammed a service cart into the abdomen of a flight attendant, causing her permanent injury.

Assailants come in all age brackets, too. After a man poured hot coffee on a flight attendant, his female companion kicked a hole in the cockpit door and with a threat that there were bombs aboard. The Bonnie-and-Clyde threats were later found to be false.

Classic Mistakes

Here is an account by a passenger aboard a Boeing-767 from New York's JFK to Cairo, Egypt.

I had a window seat and my partner sat on the aisle. After a meal and several free drinks, I dozed off. About two hours into the flight I was aroused by a commotion. A passenger seated across the aisle was attempting to open the exit door. When a flight attendant arrived, he slammed her to the floor. She yelled for help. Assistance appeared in the form of one of my traveling companions. He grabbed the man from the rear and wrestled him to the floor. He was having a hard time holding the man until my seat mate and I joined in and held his arms and feet while the flight attendant obtained plastic restraints. Here we made a mistake. We bound his hands in front, put him in his seat and fastened the safety belt. He was apologetic and seemed calm.

This demeanor lasted a few minutes---then he demanded to be released. He began crying for help. After a while he appeared to be calming down, then all hell broke loose. He had slipped the bonds on his hands and was at the cabin door. His feet were still bound so we managed to get him back on the floor. This time the captain personally attached the restraints and secured his hands behind his back. We let the arm rest down, laid the man on the seat and secured him with safety belts. This brought on the worst language you can imagine. It was so bad the flight attendant threatened to stuff a towel in his mouth. We endured this for an hour, maybe more...I lost track of the time. The captain announced we would be making an unscheduled stop in Athens, Greece. He didn't give a reason, but the flight attendants informed us the unruly passenger would be leaving the plane.

On the ground in Athens, the man made one more mistake. His bonds had been removed and he was being led from the aircraft by a Greek policeman. As the officer assisted him into the police car, the man hit him. The last we saw, the cop was playing tattoo on his head with a baton.

Two more flight attendants boarded the flight to deadhead to Cairo. One commented that the passenger had been on her flight six months before and tried the same stunt. Seems he was on medication and, when he mixed it with alcohol, became suicidal.

The captain should have never left the cockpit. What if he was seriously injured by the deranged passenger? There are too many cases of pilots going to help flight attendants in the cabin only to be attacked themselves.

An unruly passenger should always have his hands bound *behind* his back, no matter how normal or apologetic he appears when subdued. Hands bound in front can strike out at flight attendants and passengers.

The Surprise Symphony

Our last incident is not exactly air rage, but clearly shows that tolerance for disruption in the cabin is rapidly disappearing. It happened four months after September 11.

Imagine you're in a beautiful concert hall. The symphony orchestra looks fine in their tuxedo's and gowns. The maestro raises his baton and heavenly strains of Brahms fill the hall. This is pure bliss.

But on a flight across the Atlantic, 100 members of Russia's oldest, distinguished symphony orchestra caroused in such a drunken blast they were ordered off the airplane at Washington, DC, only half-way to their destination at Los Angeles. During the flight they were yelling, throwing objects around, standing in the aisles and opening their own bottles of liquor.

Because they repeatedly refused to follow the rules, the pilots and crew had the musicians and their instruments removed from the airplane. Oh yes, the airline refused to pay for their overnight stay at Dulles Airport.

Jurisdictional Gap

International and US federal law apply harsh rules for air rage perpetrators---at least on paper. Agreements were established at a 1963 Tokyo Convention, and signed by 162 countries. It's the basis by which the US prosecutes inbound offenses regardless of the carrier's nationality.

Within the US, regulations say that passengers may not interfere with an air crew. Stiff penalties up to 20 years jail are in the statutes but, as mentioned before, few disruptive passengers are prosecuted or receive harsh sentences. Part of the problem is the need to follow strict legal protocol. Passengers causing a problem must first be given notice they are in violation of federal law. Some airlines have a written warning to hand to problematic passengers and I see this as a good thing.

Notice must be given to the airline's ground operations so federal authorities can meet the aircraft. This can be a problem because the number of FBI agents assigned to major airports is limited. Smaller airports may have no federal authority at hand.

A program developed by the FBI at Detroit Metropolitan airport, the assistant US attorney and the Airline Pilots Association (ALPA) gave federal arrest authority to local law enforcement officers. Called Civil Aviation Security Enhancement (CASE), it was expanding across the country before being curtailed by the FBI's Washington DC headquarters. This was a strange decision because the CASE program was proving successful in expanding federal representation at airports with virtually no cost. There is still hope in the industry that CASE will be revived. That may be more likely now, after September 11.

Tips on Countering Air Rage

- Be prepared; discuss roles during preflight briefing.
- Communication can sometimes defuse a serious situation.
- Passenger assistance plays a pivotal, even critical, role.
- Active defense – fight back.
- Poke in the eye.
- Proper restraint devices, with hands secured behind the back.

Bad Ideas

- Communication is not appropriate in some circumstances.
- Don't leave cockpit door unlocked.
- Don't use the crash ax.
- Do not leave the perpetrator without chaperones.
- Do not leave him or her inadequately restrained.

For the Crew: Predetermined Defense

Every takeoff is prebriefed in terms of actions that might be taken if an engine fails. I am suggesting we now include a preflight discussion of what actions to take in the event of a cockpit attack. This should analyze pilot strengths and weaknesses; which pilot controls the airplane, which pilot disables the assailant.

Like all responses to inflight emergencies, awareness is critical. A pre-departure briefing should include looking around the cockpit and getting a feel for what articles may be used for defense and what objects in the cockpit inhibit freedom of movement.

The cabin crew is also be briefed on what is demanded of them in case of a cockpit attack. This includes eliciting passenger assistance as soon possible. Methods to restrain the assailant after the attack is thwarted are discussed. How will he or she be removed from the cockpit? What will tie hands and legs? Where will he or she be placed for landing?

In many cases mentioned above, the enraged passenger continued to cause havoc in the cabin once the cockpit assault was arrested. Cabin crew members are advised to tie the attacker's hand behind the back once he has been removed from the cockpit. Airlines should place handcuff straps (plastic cuffs) on board each flight as part of emergency equipment. Alternatively, duct tape is effective.

Flight Attendants are briefed to determine what each person contributes in case of a cabin attack. Each crew member should know his or her strengths and weaknesses and not be afraid to describe them to other flight attendants. If a passenger loses control and attacks a flight attendant, they become soldiers in arms.

All crew members, passengers and non-flying civilians are well advised to remember adages of combat: Never let your guard down, never underestimate your enemy.

Definitions for Air Rage
International Air Transport Association

Violence:

Any activity involving physical assault, or threat of physical assault, which is defined as an unlawful and intentional display of force against another person in such a way that it creates in the mind of that other person the belief that force is about to be used against them.

Unruly:

Any activity directed towards another person on the aircraft, passenger or crew member, that constitutes offensive, menacing or reckless behavior. For example, offensive language, verbal abuse and offensive conduct such as willful exposure are all considered prosecutable offenses.

Disruptive:

Any other unacceptable behavior Minor disturbances not including acts of violence or unruly behavior – that interfere with the comfort of fellow passengers, or interfere with the duties of crews onboard the aircraft. Examples include throwing food, defecating or urinating in the cabin.

Federal Aviation Regulations also state that "no person may assault, threaten, intimidate, or interfere with a crew member in the performance of the crew member's duties aboard an aircraft being operated."

Chapter 6

Going to School

After the September 11 attack, martial arts schools all over the U.S. noticed growing interest in self-defense courses. Interest spiked among airline passengers, professional pilots, flight attendants, military personnel and law enforcement officers. Many schools responded with specialized, short-term courses to teach how to deal with terrorists in the closed quarters of an airline cabin.

An example is the "Executive Force" program illustrated on the following pages. It was developed by In Ki Kim, who teaches at Tukong Martial Arts in Alexandria, Virginia. Kim is a Grandmaster in Tukong, developed for the South Korean Special Forces back in the 1970's.

For the executive version, no deadly moves are taught. Rather, the course is designed to subdue terrorists in the narrow confines of an airline cabin. The student is not expected to have unusual athletic ability and no uniforms are worn. As pictured on the following pages, the instruction is aimed at rushing, disarming and restraining the assailant, using the combined strength of passengers in the cabin.

Many martial arts schools developed special programs to teach self-defense to travelers. Shown here at center is Grandmaster In Ki Kim of Tukong Martial Arts in Alexandria, Virginia.

In the classroom, students are taught to grab objects like seat cushions for protection. They are advancing against knife-wielding "assailant" at the right. An important part of this and most other maneuvers is acting as a group.

After the assailant is rushed by the group and brought to the floor, a choke hold helps restrain or direct him while others tie him up.

The assailant is at the right, grabbing the passenger (wearing black). Passenger has raised arms inside, where he can use hands to strike soft parts, or grab and twist head.

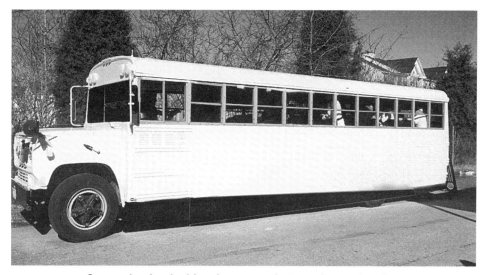

Course begins inside classroom, but continues in a former schoolbus. The bus is a more realistic simulation of the confined space of an airliner

Inside the bus, Grandmaster Kim describes techniques of self-defense for the limited space of an airplane cabin. It's important to have the passenger "pile-on" mentality to overcome assailants in close quarters. Passengers should grab "up, under and around."

Ordinary objects in an airplane can become weapons. Here, an in-flight magazine is rolled up and tightly held. Quick jabs into soft parts, using the end, can help subdue the assailant. Pens, keys and other objects may also prove effective.

Rushing a knife-wielding assailant requires skills learned in class. The untrained person, however, improves chances by grabbing a seat cushion, blanket or other object, as shown below

Grandmaster Kim demonstrates another use for a magazine. It's clamped over the face of the assailant as the knife is twisted out of the hand.

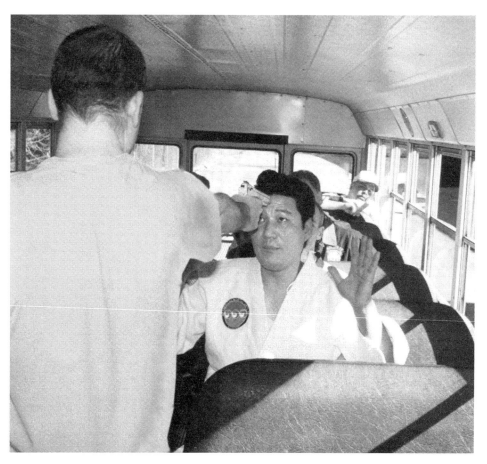

Hands raised, Grandmaster Kim demonstrates situation of gun pointed at his head. The first step, shown here, is to fake a fear response. Kim is saying, "Please, no, no, don't shoot me." This momentarily distracts the gunman, allowing a split-second for Kim to move his hands inside the assailant's arm and knock the gun to the side.

Use anything at hand, the instructor explains, to restrain
the assailant. The example being shown is a seat belt.

Chapter 7

Defending the Cockpit

There have been many proposals for hardening the cockpit against a breakthrough by a terrorist or deranged passenger. Some are controversial, such as arming pilots with guns (either deadly or non-lethal). One solution, converting the cockpit into an impregnable fortress, is already a requirement. Others envision the airplane being rescued by some kind of robot control. Whether serious or fanciful, there's no mistaking the most fundamental rule governing the flight deck; no one except pilots must ever be allowed to take over the airplane's flight controls. Let's look at what's being done to solve it.

Guns in the Cockpit

Following September 11, the US Congress passed an Airport Security bill allowing pilots to carry weapons. This includes sidearms, stun guns and pepper spray. There are two schools of thought on the subject. Opponents point out that many police officers are killed with their own guns and it's a matter of time before an innocent passenger is wounded, or worse, if pilots carry weapons. They argue that firing bullets in a confined space could wreak havoc on avionics equipment (as might a high-voltage stun gun) and possibly puncture the fuselage, depressurizing the cabin. Air marshals on board, they say, obviate the need for arming pilots. And most cockpit doors will be almost impervious to attack from the cabin, removing that route to the flight deck. The people who say pilots should not carry guns, however, are usually not pilots.

The second point of view, one I subscribe to, is a multifaceted action against terrorism. Discouraging violence in airplanes requires tough airport security, trained flight crews, reinforced cockpits, air marshals, passenger assistance and armed pilots. Why leave out the strong deterrent of arming pilots? Without doubt, if pilots are allowed to carry weapons on the flight deck they will need rigorous training.

John, a friend of mine, was a member of the Rhodesian Special Weapons Assault Team (SWAT). He advises that training pilots to carry arms should be designed to:

•Remove most, if not all, inhibitions. We are taught from childhood what is acceptable behavior. Socialized learning defines how people react in emergencies, and must be unlearned. In other words, one has to be taught to act without hesitation.

•Practice these skills until they become automatic.

•Train in simulated emergency situations until skills can be executed without conscious thought.

This regimen is designed to defend against terrorists, but isn't an enraged passenger who breaks into a cockpit with intent to injure also a terrorist? He or she may not have a political agenda, but the objective is bodily harm to pilots and, possibly, to cause the aircraft to crash. Think about a passenger aboard an Alaskan Airlines flight; as he burst into the cockpit and lunged for the controls he said, "I'm going to kill you!"

Pilot Position on Guns

The jury is still out on weapons for the crew. I know many pilots who do not agree with carrying weapons in the cockpit. Will they refuse to fly with other pilots who want to carry weapons? I hope not. To mount an effective defense against terrorists of any description, pilots must coordinate their actions.

In October 2001, a resolution circulated within the Airline Pilots Association (ALPA) asking a change in federal regulations to allow voluntary arming of flight crew members. It called for training by the FBI, licenses for concealed weapons and indemnification during legitimate use of firearms. Testifying before the House Aviation Subcommittee, ALPA said the union wanted pilots to undergo training to act as federal marshals.

Pilots are required to pass through security like everyone else and prohibited from carrying guns after an accident in 1987, when a disgruntled airline employee smuggled a gun onboard and shot both pilots. A change in attitude would be required to allow volunteer pilots to be screened and given air marshal-type training. When it looked like Congress was not going to approve pilot handguns on the flight deck, the union insisted that pilots should at least be given the right to non-lethal stun guns as a last line of defense. This option sat better with lawmakers and airline management and was finally approved. At time of writing, though, the FAA had not given its full endorsement.

Opponents to arming pilots say a deranged pilot might wreak havoc in the skies. Or a gun might be seized and used against crew members. The extreme confinement of the cockpit, too, makes it difficult to shoot an intruder entering from behind. Pilots note, however, that federal air marshals may also be picked out of the crowd, overpowered and have their guns taken. At that point, pilots would have no defense against an armed hijacker.

If an intruder breaks into a cockpit no one can tell me I cannot protect my own life. If that means having only a stun gun, so be it, but I prefer a handgun loaded with ammunition similar to that used by federal air marshals.

Before September 11, federal regulations did permit some law enforcement officers and other officials to carry weapons onboard aircraft. Even pilots had the right to carry weapons---at least in theory---as long as the airline approved. The FAA withheld permission for pilots to carry guns for many years and seems loathe to change its stance despite the green light from the new legislation.

Plastic Guns

Until security scanners are upgraded,   terrorists can smuggle non-metallic knives onboard aircraft. It stands to reason that plastic guns may also pose a problem, if such a gun could be produced. In January 1986, the Washington Post described an Austrian handgun made almost entirely of plastic. Known as the Glock 17, it's been available since 1982. The gun, however, contains over 500 grams of steel and can be easily sensed by metal detectors. Even if the gun were broken down and scattered around a person's carry-on luggage, it would be detectable by the new scanners.

Could a gun conceivably be made entirely of plastic materials? The U.S. Office of Technology Assessment foresees two types: guns made entirely of plastic and those containing some steel elements. Technology in carbon fibers, glass fibers and other composite materials could conceivably reinforce nylon or polyester plastics. Such a gun may only fire several rounds before it became inoperable, but to a terrorist that may be enough.

To make matters worse, ceramic materials now withstand high temperatures. If plastic gun barrels were protected from heat and shock by a lining of ceramic material, the life of the gun may increase considerably. There would still be a small number of metal parts, such as small springs, but these would be probably undetectable to current scanners. Like plastics, ceramics are invisible to most current X-ray scanners and metal detectors.

Concerned that undetectable guns may become available, Congress drafted legislation to make a gun illegal if it contained insufficient metal to generate a sharp X-ray image. The bill was passed with full support of the National Rifle Association. Drafting legislation may not stop a terrorist from gaining access to the latest technology in handguns. Such guns, however, may be available in the near future and become a real threat. Just another reason why airline pilots should be allowed to carry firearms.

Stun Guns

In 2001, Mesa Airlines said it would train 1,200 pilots in stun guns over three months. The airline has 800 daily departures to 153 cities. Although airline officials recognized that FAA approval was not available at that time, the program anticipated that legislation would follow.

While British Airways and other airlines mulled over whether to allow pilots to carry stun guns, in October, 2001, United Airlines announced it wanted to equip its pilots with stun guns in the cockpit. The FAA, which publicly opposed guns in cockpits, responded it would not allow pilots to carry them. But after the Airport Security Federalization Act of 2001 passed, the agency was forced to reconsider its position. Some highlights of the new law:

The weapon most often discussed for arming pilots is the Taser, which has been adopted by some airlines. The device "shoots" electrified darts at the assailant, injecting a voltage which affects the nervous system and causes uncontrollable contraction of the muscles. It disables a person despite his mental focus or physical stimulation. The Taser is effective up to about 20 feet.

The technology, known as Electro-Muscular Disruption, is not known to have caused death over the last 20 years during use by law enforcement agencies. Persons struck by the weapon have not been observed to suffer long term effects, but it is conceivable that physical stress due to narcotics or other individual anomalies might cause injury. The weapon, therefore, should be used only against extremely critical threats. (Shown is the Advance Taser M26.)

FAA may permit a pilot, co-pilot or flight engineer of a commercial aircraft who has completed training requirements to carry a firearm for protection of the aircraft.

Directs the FAA to establish a voluntary program to train and supervise commercial airline pilots.

Taser

United Airlines chose the Advance Taser, a gun used by 1,000 law enforcement agencies in North America. It is said to have four times the stopping power of other non-lethal weapons.

The FAA was worried that stun guns in the cockpit might harm avionics equipment or be seized from pilots and used against them. Another argument is that a pilot must first exit the cockpit to use a stun gun (unless the cockpit door was beaten down).

You may remember the Taser from the bungled Rodney King incident in California, where the weapon did not keep him down. Technology, however, has dramatically increased its effectiveness. Besides a traditional stun effect, the Taser is said to override the central nervous system and cause involuntary muscular contractions, disabling a person for about 15 minutes.

The Taser looks and feels like an automatic handgun. It has a laser sight for aiming up to 20 feet. Unlike the handgun or pepper spray, the Taser disables an assailant, even if struck on an arm or leg. Accurate targeting is not essential. The weapon affects the central nervous system by imitating electrical impulses within the body.

While I would like to see pilots have lethal weapons such as handguns in the cockpit, I view Tasers as an alternative to nothing at all. They appear to be effective at disarming an aggressor. But if a pilot fires, misses his target and the probes (emitted by the Taser) hit a circuit breaker or instrument panel, there may be interesting effects on avionics systems. The possibility of electrical anomalies are real, but, in my opinion, the risk of not having a device to stop a cockpit intruder far outweighs electrical and instrument malfunctions.

Struggle in the Cockpit

Let's assume the pilots are not carrying weapons. Before consider-
ing moves to disable an assailant, look at the environment where
pilots need to defend themselves. Some cockpits are larger than
others, and crew size varies between short and long haul flights,
yet there are common elements:

Both pilots sit facing forward with seat belts fastened. On
departure and approach, shoulder harnesses also restrain movement. Pilots' legs are usually on either side of the control yoke
(or wheel). Airbus aircraft usually have a small side-stick controller off to one side, which replaces the control yoke.

While a pilot's hands are free to "dial and press" controls, his
or her arms have limited freedom of movement, which greatly reduces the force behind a blow a pilot can deliver against an attacker.

Most people are right-handed.

Most first officers (the co-pilot) are younger than captains.

Men are usually stronger than women.

Given the last three facts, male first officers will probably
provide the best defense against an attack on the cockpit. If the
first officer (and/or captain) is a woman, she shouldn't think that
being female will divert an attacker's intent to harm her. If she is
the last line of defense, she should be prepared to fight dirty with
every ounce of her strength.

The following example is a next-to-worst-case scenario: an
abrupt attack on the cockpit by an unarmed, enraged, large-framed
male. Keep in mind that while the following scenario and defenses
refer to a male assailant, the attacker may be an enraged female
passenger. The same defenses apply in either case.

The captain is enjoying a cup of coffee, discussing with his
first officer where they might eat dinner that night, when a flight
attendant calls on the interphone. She says there's a problem with
a loud, abusive passenger.

Pilots should not leave the cockpit under any circumstances.

Instead, they take the call for what it is: a heads-up. Each
pilot loosens the seatbelt and considers sliding one or both seats
back to gain maximum range of movement. They briefly discuss
their roles should an intruder enter the cockpit. They mentally

prepare for combat.

Five minutes later, the captain is about to call the cabin for an update on the unruly passenger when the cockpit door bursts open. A 200-pound enraged man crashes into the cockpit. He screams obscenities and grabs for controls. The captain's heart races, he's nervous, his blood pressure goes through the roof. Although he prepared for this, over several precious moments he is stunned by the intrusion. Body chemistry, though, is arming him with what he needs to defend against the intruder: adrenaline.

Since the attacker may have no idea how to shut down an engine, he may attempt to interfere with the thrust levers (throttles), control column or both. The attack's suddenness and ferocity are disorienting, but the pilots spring into action.

The captain focuses on one objective: keeping the man's hands away from the controls. He grabs the assailant's fingers and bends them back, or uses finger nails to scratch deeply into flesh. If he has the opportunity, the pilot may fly the airplane into a severe maneuver to throw the assailant off balance. The captain or first officer should, if possible, use the public address system to call for assistance from the passenger cabin. If that's not possible, they should scream "Help" at the top of their lungs. Both pilots should yell as much as possible to destabilize their opponent, bolster their courage and give maximum strength to their attack.

The first officer strikes aggressively and repeatedly as soon as the assailant comes through the cockpit door. This may not only disable him, but divert attention from grabbing the controls. The copilot will not stop his or her attack on the assailant until help arrives from the cabin and the aggressor is removed from the cockpit. The emphasis is on aggressive defense.

It is imperative for the first officer to strike the attacker as many times as he or she can and with all possible strength, even while being struck by the assailant. If necessary, and if the assailant redirects focus away from control of the airplane, the captain joins the fray.

This point is critical: Pilots should not hit him once and hope he'll be discouraged from continuing the attack; the man is supercharged with adrenaline, and possibly other chemical substances, and may not react to painful strikes. In other words, blows may only enrage him further if they diminish during the counterattack.

Flight Attendants

Because flight attendants bear the responsibility of spotting problem passengers, they are the first line of defense. Well before the incident described above, it is essential that they participate in a preflight briefing with pilots, and establish a defense strategy. Items to discuss before flight include strengths and weaknesses of individuals, coded messages to pass to each other if support is needed and what cabin items may thwart physical attacks. If a passenger becomes enraged, for example, and the flight attendant feels threatened, the message might be:

"Jan, do you have any bottled water in the galley?"

If the attacker is armed, a different message is required. Something like:

"Jan, could you get more coffee from the front, please?"

Hearing this, Jan immediately knows her buddy is warning of a possible explosive situation. She goes to the galley, informs the pilots and other flight attendants by interphone and, depending on her threat assessment, enlists male passengers to assist if the situation deteriorates.

A coded message should be established with pilots about how to inform them that a flight attendant is being forced by an armed passenger to call the cockpit. Any sentence or word suffices so long as it's incongruent with normal communication. I know one airline uses the sentence:

"Captain, I must come to the cockpit."

The sentence, with subtle emphasis on *must*, is not unusual enough to raise suspicions in an enraged passenger, but tells pilots that a flight attendant is being forced to bring an armed passenger into the cockpit.

Armed passengers must never be admitted to the cockpit. To guard against it, any crew member, whether operating deadhead or in a jumpseat, should be required to give his or her cockpit key to the captain for safe keeping. This places flight attendants in the unenviable position of knowing their lives are at extreme risk if an armed passenger attacks and demands access to the cockpit.

Despite feelings of anxiety and guilt, pilots will no longer open the cockpit door, even if it means the imminent death of a crew member.

If a situation can be defused by communication techniques it may avoid a nasty situation. As incidents in this book illustrate, however, when a passenger appears to regain composure it does not mean he or she will not flare up again. Flight attendants must assume that a passenger who created a disturbance on one occasion will become problematic again, and the crew proceeds according to strategy discussed in advance. It is wise to seat the passenger well away from emergency exits or entry doors and enlist the assistance of male passengers to monitor his behavior.

Restraining the Assailant

Pilots and flight attendants should brief together and separately on what actions they will demand during a cockpit or cabin assault. This should include pilots reminding flight attendants to elicit passenger assistance as soon possible. How will he or she be removed from the cockpit? How will hands and legs be tied? Where will he or she be placed for landing?

In actual cases, one enraged passenger continued to cause havoc in the cabin once the cockpit assault was stopped. Cabin crew members, therefore, should tie the attacker's hands behind his or her back after removal from the cockpit. To this end, airlines must place plastic cuffs or similar restraining devices on board each flight---preferably within easy reach of flight attendants---as part of the emergency equipment. The cheapest and possibly most effective restraint might be as simple as duct tape.

Flight attendants and pilots are well advised to remember adages of combat: Never let your guard down, never underestimate your enemy.

Smart Autopilot

Let's assume the cockpit has been breached and terrorists are in command. Some experts argue that airplanes can be prevented from crashing into buildings by modifying the autopilot. The technique would tie into a system called TAWS, for Terrain Avoidance Warning System. The obstruction-warning device will be installed aboard most airliners. Another suggestion would modify the autopilot so controllers on the ground could take over a hijacked plane and keep it in the air until order is restored.

Yet another idea is an irreversible "hijack switch" that turns control over to the airplane's Flight Management System (FMS), which then guides the airplane to the nearest airport to land automatically.

None of these ideas are practical for the foreseeable future. First, only 53 airports in the U.S. are certified for automatic landings. Even if a commercial jet is equipped, it still needs a human pilot to determine which runway to use, assess weather conditions and whether the runway is operational or closed. Pilots still need to manually dial in settings, such as final approach course, then fly the aircraft until the course is captured. They manually engage autothrottles and lower landing gear and flaps. There are other problems; hijackers could shut down engines in flight or switch off electrical systems. The "smart" landing is simply unworkable today.

Ground Control

Taking over control of the airplane from the ground also is not a good idea. Having someone on the ground fly a jetliner full of passengers is not viable. There would have to be qualified pilots on reserve at all times in air traffic control facilities across the country. Any other option is ludicrous. Would you want an untrained person on the ground remotely flying your plane in crowded airways? Not only that, it introduces another hijack possibility. Ground control centers would have to be heavily guarded, their commands sent over secure, jam-proof data links.

Despite lapses in judgment and human error, people are still the best option for solving difficult situations. Computers are great at predictable scenarios, but throw in the unanticipated curve ball and the system goes "tilt". Pilots must be the ultimate authority when it comes to controlling the aircraft. What is more, autopilots work best when a human monitors every maneuver, ready to take over if something untoward occurs.

Blast-proof Cargo Compartments

PanAm 103 exploded at 31,000 feet over Lockerbie, Scotland 38 minutes after taking off from London. Two hundred and seventy people were killed, including 11 on the ground. In the investigation, authorities found fragments of a circuit board and timer, deducing the cause as terrorism. A law professor at the University of Glasgow, John Grant, declared the PanAm crash was the largest case of mass murder in the world. It was--- before September 11.

Investigators determined that Semtex plastic explosives were planted on PanAm in a cassette recorder hidden in a suitcase. The bag originated on an Air Malta flight headed from Malta's Luqa airport to Frankfurt, Germany, where it was transferred to a PanAm flight going to London. The bag was transferred to PanAm 103 in London and placed in the forward cargo hold. After the tragedy, aircraft manufacturers, airlines and aviation authorities began an intense study in reinforcing cargo areas to withstand bomb blasts.

Boeing noted there were 34 inflight bombing attempts between 1971 and 1995, with fifteen proving catastrophic. Of those fifteen, 7 were lost to structural damage, 3 to systems failure and 2 to undetermined flight impairment.

Bombings against commercial aviation are worldwide. Throughout the last 30 years, 33 countries and 40 airlines fell victim to terrorist attacks of this sort. The good news is that 56% of the aircraft survived inflight bombings, with wide-body aircraft having a better rate than narrow bodies. Seventy-three percent of wide-body aircraft survived bomb blasts as compared to 48% of narrow bodies. This was mainly due to greater internal volume to absorb the blast, more structural surface to dissipate blast loads and greater aircraft systems redundancy and separation. The bad news is, terrorists are building new bombs of sophisticated material that may be more difficult to detect.

Boeing conducted blast tests in actual aircraft to determine the main areas of impact and how airplanes could be reinforced to survive. El Al appears to be the only airline to heed the warning by installing blast-proof cargo compartments. Other airlines resisted this route, presumably because of cost, downtime, installation and increased fuel burns due to added weight. It is cheaper, some say, to be sure a bomb can't get on an airplane rather than protect against inflight blast.

Bomb-proofing the cargo compartment, however, may not be necessary. Nearly all aircraft carry baggage in containers loaded into cargo holds. Some designs are able to withstand the force of a blast. One company, Galaxy Aviation Security, has developed a hardened baggage container that can contain the force of an explosion. Weighing approximately 300 pounds it is constructed of lightweight, high strength, damage-tolerant panels that, because of modular design, can be changed in the field using ordinary tools. The containers have a metal frame and a door sealed by a damage-tolerant mechanism. Airlines should consider the design because it falls within the weight criteria and handling abilities of non-blast proof containers in use today.

Blast tests of the container were carried out by the FAA and the product proved it could protect an airframe from suffering significant structural damage. In fact, the container itself suffered no significant damage other than deformed side panels. This planned reaction to the blast actually makes damage inspection easier because impact damage is visible first on the outside of the container.

Boeing and Airbus announced after September 11 that new aircraft in the next few years, such as the double-decker A-380, will be modified. Two approaches under consideration are blast-proof cargo holds and strengthened fuselages.

Fortified Cockpit Doors

Reinforcing cockpit doors was mandated by Congress in 2001. At the time of writing, U.S. airlines had installed lock bars or stronger latches as an interim measure. In an incident mentioned earlier, a passenger kicked an opening in the bottom of a door which had been reinforced with a metal crossbar, and poked his head into the cockpit. Reinforcing bars will be replaced by far stronger systems.

The FAA called for permanent cockpit reinforcement and changes in procedures for flight and cabin crew to restrict cockpit access. The agency gave airlines 6 months to come up with complete cockpit design changes. Federal grants up to $500 million would help airlines upgrade to bulletproof and bombproof doors.

Door leading to the cockpit must be hardened to prevent entry. The one shown here, fitted to an Air Alaska B-727, is opened and closed by remote control from inside the cockpit. (Courtesy, Raisbeck Engineering.)

84

In contrast to flimsy, pre-September 11 doors, the new one resists battering down.

The door must also be bulletproof, accomplished with two 1-1/4-inch thick bullet-proof glass windows. In this demonstration, five .44 Magnum bullets were fired point blank at James Raisbeck. CEO. He said, "We stand behind our product."

Before September 11, cockpit doors were intentionally "break-away" to allow rescuers to reach disabled pilots. The new fortified doors will still meet certain requirements, such as not hindering evacuation, equalization of cabin pressure in case of decompression and provisions to open the door from both sides.

One manufacturer, Raisbeck Engineering, signed a contract with Alaskan Airlines in October 2001 to install hardened cockpit security for a fleet of Boeing 737 aircraft. The door also anticipates future regulations, such as bullet-proofing and increased awareness by the pilots of what's happening in the passenger cabin. It has observation windows in the door made of bullet-proof glass, which can be augmented with video surveillance. The door weighs approximately 48 pounds and withstands 1500 pounds of force.

Another company, TTF Aerospace, had been developing a cockpit door that would be impervious to air rage attacks. After September 11, the company made modifications to make the door impervious to bullet penetration. TTF's armored cockpit door includes a light-weight core reinforced by layers of composite materials that resist knife blade and ballistic attack, while complying with smoke, burn and toxicity regulations. The door is finished with fiberglass sheets resembling a factory-fitted cockpit door. It weighs 75 pounds and costs about $9000. In comparison, a standard cockpit door costs $6,000 and weighs about 40 pounds. TTF hardens areas around the cockpit door, and uses a strengthened latch and keyless door opening from the outside. To comply with FAA regulations, the door can be removed quickly from inside the cockpit by a removable spring-loaded hinge.

Video Monitors

While the Aviation Security Act of 2001 calls for video monitors to alert pilots to suspicious activity in the cabin, some suggest adding a video recorder. Investigators could then view what happened in an accident from any cause, including hijacking.

The airplane's existing Flight Data Recorder (FDR) stores altitude, airspeed, heading and, in later models, control positions and other information. The Cockpit Voice Recorder (CVR) records pilot voice communications with Air Traffic Control and with each other. It also picks up audible sounds in the cockpit on an area microphone. This provides investigators with a valuable record of voices, engine noise, flap handle movement, landing gear extension and audible warnings.

Both recorders---often called "the black boxes"---are crash-survivable, mounted in the tail and equipped with an underwater locator beacon. After an accident, they are transferred to Washington, DC and analyzed by experts from the NTSB, FAA, the airline, aircraft manufacturer, engine manufacturer and pilot unions. They transcribe the tapes and compare the data with ATC voice and radar tapes to establish time lines.

When pilots are trained in flight simulators, video cameras are often in the cockpit to assess crew performance. The tapes are usually erased after a review with instructors. It's easy to transfer this technology to an actual aircraft and install a video recorder constructed like the aircraft's flight data and cockpit voice recorders. Having a video record of pilot actions, or images of who interfered with the airplane, is invaluable for figuring out what happened before an accident. Imagine how investigators would have benefitted if such systems were aboard the airliners in the September 11 attack.

Chapter 8

Smoke, Fire and Evacuation

Passengers evacuate airliners on the average *once every 11 days*. But rising out of your seat and heading toward an exit is considered a rare event. There are more than 30,000 departures in the U.S. every day, so your chances of an evacuation are 1 in 1 million.

Most evacuations do not result from crashes but some condition that alarms the crew, such as the smell of smoke or a landing gear that's stuck. The danger is rarely immediate, but the flight crew deems it wise to evacuate before docking at the gate---just in case the damage is escalating.

If the airplane is downed by a catastrophe, however, noxious fumes and spreading fire demand a rapid evacuation. Getting out of the airplane and surviving often depends on knowing what to do during precious moments measured in seconds.

Looking for Trouble

During the 1990's, the National Transportation Safety Board took a novel approach in investigating accidents. Before then, researchers had studied only what went *wrong* in a crash. There was a meticulous search for the subtlest clue in the wreckage---a burn pattern, a scrape mark, a fracture line. From careful observations they develop a "probable cause"---and have solved nearly every airline accident. But a wealth of data had gone unnoticed. After most crashes, a certain number of passengers escape with little or no injury---yet no one had asked them why.

To find the answers, NTSB investigated 46 accidents involving 2,651 passengers over a two-year period in the 1990's. After interviewing flight attendants, flight crews and passengers, the Safety Board generated surprising new information—and issued 23 safety recommendations to the FAA.

Two severe accidents dramatically affirmed the Board's approach. A Boeing-737 collided with commuter aircraft on the runway at Los Angeles. All passengers on the commuter died on impact. Not one passenger on the 737, however, died from the collision—but 19 expired from smoke inhalation. Here is where the Board's persistence shed new light on what happened in the seconds after the collision. Of the 19 who perished from smoke, more than half were lined up in the aisle trying to reach an exit. The Board also discovered that lifesaving seconds were lost as passengers failed to open the exit door in time. Another delay occurred when a scuffle broke out between two passengers. These revelations began to challenge the belief that everyone dies instantly in an airplane crash.

Deadly Unfamiliarity

In the other accident, a commuter aircraft, seconds after landing at an Illinois airport, struck a King Air (business aircraft). Twelve people aboard the commuter were still alive after the impact, but were killed by smoke and fumes in the post-crash fire.

This accident was a double tragedy. The first rescuers to reach the burning aircraft ran toward the cockpit to pull out the pilots. The captain, still inside the airplane, desperately asked rescuers to get the forward door open. The rescuers fought to open the door but couldn't get it open. Within minutes, the two pilots perished in the flames.

The shocking conclusion was that rescuers were familiar with the airplane, but the Safety Board determined that instructions for opening the door were not clear enough to follow in an emergency. Not long after, the FAA ordered new instructions for all exits on that model aircraft. Again, the killer was not the crash, but the deadly conditions which ensued. Maybe there were remedies, the Board concluded, to reduce the toll of death and injury.

90 Seconds to Go

To certify a new airplane, passengers and crew must be able to get out and be on the ground in 90 seconds or less. The FAA may require the manufacturer to run a full-scale demonstration with crew and "passengers" (actually hired hands or volunteers) under difficult conditions of darkness, all seats occupied and half the emergency exits blocked.

Airplane makers have criticized such full-scale demonstrations because they may prove dangerous. They are also costly: a full-scale demo in the late 1990's cost over $1 million. Injuries do, in fact, occur in simulated evacuations, but they also reveal problems in the procedure.

Evacuation Pitfalls

Knowing how to use an evacuation slide is important because passenger injuries while using the slide are not uncommon. But there are other reasons. Demonstrating that passengers can get out of the airplane in 90 seconds applies only to aircraft with 44 or more passenger seats. These larger airplanes have flight attendants who's major responsibility is to guide you out of the airplane in an emergency. Commercial aircraft with fewer than 20 seats, however, may not have flight attendants on board. Now, the pilots become your guide in the event of an emergency and they might not be available to you in the cabin.

The lesson is simple. Always be ready to evacuate on your own and be familiar with procedures we'll describe in a moment.

Several emergency exit types are shown in the illustration and, according to FAA regulations, opening them "...must be simple and obvious and not require exceptional effort." Crew members practice operating those doors at least every two years, but most passengers never gain that experience until a real evacuation. Be prepared to find an alternate route if the exit doesn't function. After a crash in Little Rock, Arkansas, the seats in an MD-82 broke

PASSENGER EMERGENCY EXITS COME IN VARIOUS SIZES

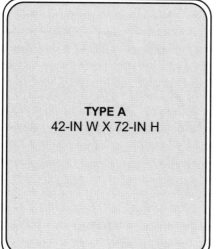

TYPE A
42-IN W X 72-IN H

Largest door, six feet high, has passageways from the aisles. This door is equipped with a two-lane emergency slide. If the door is over a wing and there is a step-down outside, the slide typically deploys automatically and reaches the ground.

Doors below often have "step-up" limits, which is the distance from the airplane floor to the door sill. The "step-down" is how far you step down outside the airplane.

Always check the information provided on the safety card and signs.

TYPE III
20-IN W
X 36-IN H

TYPE I
24-IN W X 48-IN H

Floor level exit

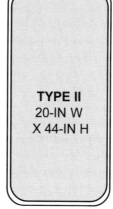

TYPE II
20-IN W
X 44-IN H

Most often placed over the wing, with a step-down not to exceed 36 inches. Step-up not to exceed 20 inches.

Floor level exit. May be located over the wing, with step-up inside the aiplane of no more than10 inches and step- down outside the airplane not exceeding 27 inches.

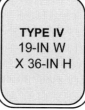

TYPE IV
19-IN W
X 36-IN H

Over-the-wing exit. The step-up can be no greater than 29 inches, the step-down no greater than 36 inches

free and blocked the aisles. The floor was severely deformed and overhead bins fell down. But working in your favor is the FAA requirement that you should be able to get in 90 seconds with *half* the exits blocked.

The researchers also report some encouraging news. After interviewing scores of passengers who lived through severe crashes, they found that most were able to pick their away around obstacles. Also, emergency exits may not be the only way to get out of an aircraft. It is not unusual for a crash to split open the airframe at several points. Passengers can often exit through the gaps.

Get Up and Go

You should neither assume nor await the assistance of crewmembers. They are trained to operate emergency equipment but are not always available. According to the NTSB, exits over the wings are "expected to be and will primarily be opened by passengers." A flight attendant may be assigned to open an overwing exit but the Board discovered that passengers are more likely to be the first to open overwing exits because flight attendants may not be near them.

Except in a few cases where the airplane is seriously deformed in a crash, blocking some exits, passengers have proven successful in getting doors and hatches open. But it doesn't always go smoothly. In a crash at Atlanta, a woman was unable to open a hatch and stood aside for another passenger, who succeeded. In Chicago aboard a 727, passengers reported "struggling to maneuver the heavy exit"---and throw it out the airplane.

In Manchester, England, during evacuation of a 737, a passenger at a window exit tried to open the hatch. Unfortunately, the passenger was pulling on the *seat arm*. Another passenger reached over and pulled the correct release but the hatch fell inward, trapping the first passenger. By the time the hatch was tossed out of the way, 45 seconds had elapsed from the time the aircraft stopped rolling. These moments are often a matter of life and death. In another accident, passengers worked quickly, successfully releasing a window exit 6 seconds *before* the aircraft came to a stop.

In one MD-82 accident, a 22-year-old passenger operated

the release handle of an overwing exit and pushed. The door didn't budge so he put his shoulder against it and pushed. He was unaware that harder you push an airplane door, the tighter the fit. It's designed that way to contain pressurized air in the cabin--and one more reason you must open the door according to instructions.

Figure It Out

These incidents touch on one of the hottest issues in aircraft design; "human factors." It raises the question, are these doors too complex for ordinary people to operate? Or is it the passengers' fault for not reading the placards? And what about opening a door while inside a burning plane?

If a passenger attempts to figure out the exit door on his own, the task is daunting. Some hatches must be first unlocked, then turned. Next, it is placed on the seat---or thrown out of the opening. Such maneuvering, experts say, is difficult to illustrate on a placard. They point out that there is a large number of successful door openings by passengers, but emergency exits need improvement.

Qualified Passenger

An early solution was a federal law requiring "qualified" passengers to be seated next to exits. It says a passenger must be able to:
- Locate and operate the emergency exit
- Assess conditions outside an exit
- Follow instructions of crewmembers
- Open and stow the exit hatch
- Assess the condition of and stabilize a slide
- Pass quickly through an exit
- Decide and act quickly---without prior training.

Whether you sit next to an emergency exit as a qualified passenger, or are seated somewhere else, there is a proven way to greatly increase your chances of survival:

Know how to open the emergency exit.

NTSB states the problem directly; "Passenger inattention to safety materials provided". Air carriers must display pictorial instructions, not only on the safety briefing card (in the seat back), but at each emergency exit. The procedure may appear confusing, but usually can be understood in a few minutes by studying the words and pictures, step-by-step. If you are seated next to an emergency exit, a flight attendant will probably approach you and ask if you understand the procedure. It may be worth your life and those of other passengers to ask for a quick explanation if the instructions aren't clear.

An actual incident, a collision on the runway at Los Angeles, shows how the briefing paid off. Before departure, a flight attendant questioned the passenger seated next an emergency exit, asking if he could fulfill the duties of an able-bodied person in the event of an emergency. He replied he was 17 years old. To be certain he understood his responsibilities, the flight attendant also briefed passengers around the young man's row. In later interviews with survivors after the collision, her actions had provided valuable information that speeded the evacuation.

Future aircraft may lessen the confusion of opening an exit. Boeing designed a new exit hatch for its 737 aircraft which opens outward, the intuitive or expected direction. The passenger does not have to decide whether to stow or throw out the hatch because it swings up out of the way. But this new human-factors design may not appear throughout the entire airline fleet for many years.

Lighting the Way

Because darkness and smoke interfere with passengers reaching exits, government regulations require emergency illumination independent of the airplane's regular lighting. Not only are the cabin and exits illuminated, there is a path of lights along the floor. An alternate location for these lights is on the side of the seat near the aisle. Ever since such illumination became a requirement, they've proved their value. In 30 real-life accidents, lighting systems failed only once during an emergency evacuation.

The low, in-floor location of lights exploits the principle that hot gases rise. Although smoke may billow through the cabin, there is a chance that getting yourself low to the floor may help you find clearer air and a better view of the path illuminated by the escape lighting. Where the lights reach an exit, their color

Research by the NTSB indicates that passengers may have difficulty handling emergency exits (if the flight crew is not available to open them). Doors may be heavy, awkward to lift or maneuver while opening. There may also be confusion on where to stow the door, inside or out of the airplane. Always carefully follow instructions on the door.

The rules also require that a passenger seated next to an emergency exit be qualified to perform the task (usually by answering questions from the flight attendant or reading the sign).

A new generation of emergency doors, based on human factors, is expected to solve that problem. As shown in the illustration above, it is hinged at the top. By swinging up, it needs little handling or stowing. The door is already on late-model B-737's.

The design of the new door was a response by the airplane-maker to the European Joint Aviation Authorities (similar to the U.S. FAA). The new-model airplane was designed to carry more passengers, but the European authority agreed only if there was a change in cabin design, in this case, the improved, swing-up emergency door.

changes, typically from white to red, but check the safety card for the details.

Count the Rows

People in the aviation industry have devised their own method of finding the exit if cabin visibility drops to zero They count the number of seat backs between their seat and the exit when first boarding the airplane. In an emergency, with no guiding lights, you can touch the seat backs to count your way to the exit.

Over the Seats

An obstacle to a fast escape, researchers found, is debris from the aircraft interior falling into the aisle. You may see an exit many feet away, but the route is impassable. Trying to clear a path by lifting obstructions could waste time or be impossible. Don't fixate on the aisle as the only route. If another exit is not accessible, you may get a clear shot to an exit by crawling over the *tops* of the seats.

Smoke

Because noxious gases (not burns) are the leading cause of death in a fire, there have been numerous recommendations for passengers to be supplied with smoke hoods. They provide precious minutes of breathing during evacuation. They're not available on aircraft at this time, but you can purchase your own. Be wary of very inexpensive smoke hoods (about $10) because they may not function well.

Another tactic for traversing a smoky cabin is to cover your mouth with a material, such as a pillow case or headrest cover. Wet it if you can. Get your head down low to find clearer air.

Look for the Light

After a crash, survivors often report seeing daylight through cracks in the fuselage. In many instances, they unbuckle their seat belt and step out through the opening. Be cautious and avoid any route where flames make it impassable.

A life-saving system is in-floor emergency lighting. If the cabin fills with smoke the lights can lead you to an emergency exit. Note that the trail of lights along the aisle are white. They end at a red light which indicates where to turn for the emergency exit (which also has red illumination).

Placing the lights low exploits the fact that hot gases rise. If visibility is poor in the cabin, it may be clearer near the floor. Thus, it might be necessary to get down and crawl to get a good view of the lighting.

Always verify the lighting by checking the safety card; in some aircraft, the lights are up somewhat higher, on or near the seat arms.

These lights have proven very reliable during actual incidents. They operate on their own battery power, independent of other electrical systems on the airplane.

Sliding off the Airplane

Once you've gotten past the emergency exit, you're only halfway to safety. If the exit is higher than six feet above ground, the FAA requires some kind of assistance to get you to down quickly and safely. It may be rubbery bridge to the ground known as an evacuation slide. According to the rules, it must deploy and be ready within 6 seconds (10 seconds, for some types) and support itself---even if the airplane's landing gear collapses.

Slides, though, have proved troublesome. In a review of 19 actual situations, there were seven instances where slides did not operate as expected. In some instances, maintenance people had failed to fill the inflation bottle. In others, the slide material jammed the mechanism, or the operating lanyard was not attached. Some slides were labeled "automatic," but could be inflated only manually. Early in the year 2000, the FAA convened a task group to correct these deficiencies.

Today the major hazard of evacuation is not malfunctioning slides. They've actually caused few serious injuries. Passengers are more frequently hurt when they jump out of exits or off the wings. In one evacuation from a B-727 in Ft. Lauderdale, Florida, a dozen passengers got out and began moving toward the wingtip. A crewmember had to herd them back to the rear of the wing where they could slide down. In other instances, passengers stood on the wing near the slide and interfered with others trying to escape.

Surprisingly, most serious injuries occurred where *no* slide was required---where the wing is less than 6 feet above ground. This is true of the B-727 and B-737, which together comprise most of the world's airline fleet. The Safety Board pressed the FAA to re-examine whether six feet is too high without helping the passenger down.

Smoke hoods are designed to filter toxic gases that may fill the cabin after a fire. The model shown provides up to 20 minutes of escape time. The hood resists temperatures up to 800 degrees F to protect eyes, head and neck from flames.

These devices have been opposed by the airlines as too expensive to provide for each passenger. FAA contends that putting on a smoke hood may delay getting out of the airplane. The European Transport Safety Council, on the other hand, conducted a study and concluded that smoke hoods should be provided on all commercial aircraft. Because of wide publicity in the media, passengers are buying their own (like the "Evac-U8" model pictured above) and taking them when they fly.

Most Fortune 500 companies equip their corporate aircraft with smoke hoods and the U.S. Air Force has purchased over 34,000 of them. *(Photo courtesy of Brookdale International Systems of Vancouver, B.C., Canada.)*

Planned and Unplanned Evacuations

There are several reasons for evacuating an airplane but the leading threat is smoke or fire inside or outside the airplane. (Stuck landing gear also ranks high.) They trigger two types of evacuation; planned and unplanned. In the former, the airplane is cruising aloft, allowing time for the crew to brief you on the bracing position, and how and when to use the emergency exits. Trained flight attendants direct passengers to sit near overwing exits, then remain near them to be sure they're opened quickly. Passengers are told to remove hazardous objects.

Another benefit of the planned evacuation is that it's stretched out in time. Passengers aboard one commuter aircraft, for example, were surprised when the flight attendant said there were no evacuation slides outside the exit. She explained they were not required. In another incident, passengers were surprised to learn there were slides at the exit; they had expected stairs.

In the aftermath of a planned evacuation the crew is often applauded. When passengers are safely on the ground, they remark; "No one panicked...we were well informed...the crew deserves medals."

Then there are *unplanned* evacuations. They happen when a stricken airplane is low to, or on, the ground. Now there is little time to learn procedures and mentally scope out an escape. To make matters worse, *most* evacuations are unplanned. In one accident review, researchers found there were three times as many unplanned evacuations, occurring just after the airplane was taxiing, taking off or landing---compared with about one-third such incidents aloft.

Jump---Don't Sit

The airplane is now stopped and you're at the emergency hatch, ready to exit. If there is a slide for descending to the ground, you should not use the children's playground method for going down the slide. You should not first *sit* at the top of the slide, then push off. That wastes time and doesn't allow enough people to exit the airplane in the specified time (70 people must be able to slide down

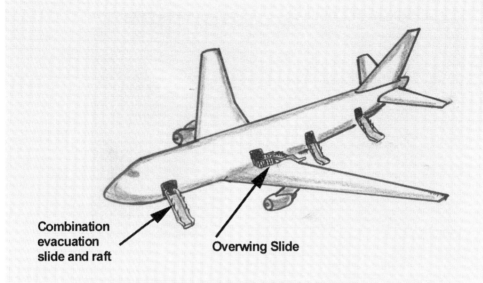

Combination
evacuation
slide and raft

Overwing Slide

Getting out of the airplane may require the evacuation slide. Be sure to read the details on the safety card or at the exit. Some slides inflate automatically, some are triggered manually. Near the nose of the airplane, in the illustration above, the slide also contains a raft in the event of a ditch-ing. Another slide shown is an overwing type.

If you're out on the wing, try to use the slide to avoiding jumping from the wing to the ground. The correct way to enter the slide is to *jump* off the door frame and land on the slide on your buttocks. If you merely sit down and push off, precious time will be wasted.

In many aircraft, there is no slide at the exit because the wing is less than 6 feet above the ground (for example, the B-727 and B-737, which comprise most of the fleet). At this height, however, jumping off can cause injury, so lower yourself carefully from the wing.

a lane every minute). The method, therefore, is "jump and slide." Although leaping out of the airplane seems daunting, jumping causes few serious injuries.

Safety Briefing: *Ho-hum*

It's hardly news that most passengers do not listen to the whole safety briefing. The reasons given;

> Saw it before
> It's basic knowledge
> Reading
> Sleeping
> Distracted by other person or child
> Listening to music
> Too long

Passengers who lived through actual evacuations were divided on the briefing's effectiveness. The main complaint was the briefing covered situations that didn't apply. They wanted more information on the route to the exit and how to slide or get off a wing. For 25 years the industry was urged to devise better ways to communicate safety information to passengers but improvement has been slow.

In addition to boredom, inattentive passengers increase their risk. Not only are there differences in airplane models, but variations in exit types, routes and other safety devices.

Safety cards in the seatback pocket suffer much the same inattention as the briefing from the flight attendant.   By law, the card contains details and diagrams on doors, slides and other features of the specific airplane you're riding on.

Although safety cards contain essential information you need to survive, researchers find that comprehension level among passengers is dismally low. The quality of instructions vary widely and illustrations for opening are not often clarified by enlargements or use of color. Some are not clear on how to get off a wing or whether to put the escape hatch inside or out. Because many cards do not explicitly depict information, the Safety Board has urged that companies which prepare the cards, test them for passenger comprehension, not a requirement at this writing.

Carry-On Doesn't Mean Carry-Off

In a remarkable number of emergencies, the evacuation is slowed by passengers insisting on taking their carry-on baggage. When quizzed later, many said the preflight briefing should include an instruction to "Leave everything." Most people, in fact, left the airplane with their bags. Items of value often mentioned are wallets, credit cards, money, keys and medicine. Are they worth a life?

The reason for grabbing bags is the perception that once the airplane stops, the emergency is over. The cabin appears normal, with no sign of fire or smoke. But this is no guarantee that jet fuel hasn't saturated the ground, or electrical circuits haven't overheated.

The greatest single blockage to evacuating the airplane, in fact, is carry-on luggage. It has even caused arguments between passenger and flight attendant. Nearly one-half the passengers who had to evacuate an airplane agreed that carry-on baggage had slowed the flow. One grandmother wisely persuaded her grandchildren to leave their toys and coloring book behind. Their departure down the aisle, however, was slowed by another passenger trying to get luggage down from and overhead bin. Another passenger reported he couldn't get out quickly because someone was trying to push a large garment bag through the overwing exit. One flight attendant had to throw bags out the opening because they cluttered the exit.

The Torch

If you fly the B-727, the second-most common airliner in the world, you could encounter the "torch". One evening at Chicago O'Hare, after passengers had boarded, the crew started the Auxiliary Power Unit. It's a small jet engine near the tail that generates power for air conditioning and starting the main engines.

A bright orange flame from the rear flashed along the right side of the airplane, past cabin windows. Passengers screamed "Fire" and ran to an emergency exit on the left side. The captain ordered passengers to remain seated, but in the evacuation , a 10-year-old boy broke his arm jumping off the wing. Several other passengers were also injured.

Why Passengers Are Inattentive
to Safety Briefings

Reasons Given	Percent
Passenger had seen safety briefing previously	54.0
Passenger believed content was common knowledge	15.3
Passenger was reading during safety briefing	6.1
Passenger said view of safety briefing was obstructed	2.2
Passenger was distracted by another person (not child)	1.8
Passenger distracted by child	0.4
Passenger listening to recorded music	0.2
Passenger said briefing was too long	0.2
Other reasons	9.6

The National Transportation Safety Board surveyed 457 passengers who experienced an emergency evacuation between 1997 and 1999. As shown in the right-hand column, most (54%) said they had seen it previously. For this and other reasons, the Safety Board said; "We really have not made progress in getting people to watch these safety briefings." It urged the aviation industry to come up with innovative ways to attract attention and communicate vital, life-saving information.

In airline parlance, this is an "uncommanded evacuation". And it was unnecessary because the reason was a "torching APU". It is not uncommon (or dangerous) for the Auxiliary Power Unit to accumulate fuel and ignite a brief plume of fire on starting. In the 727, passengers saw it over the right wing and believed the airplane was on fire.

To allay such fears, airlines were urged to announce a warning over the PA system before starting the APU. That recommendation, however, was never mandated by law.

Two overwing exits are seen removed for an evacuation. The doors are lying on the wing. Some doors must be thrown out of the airplane, others are not. The exact details of how to stow the door (that is, dispose of it) are shown on or near the door.

There have been evacuations where passengers were delayed from exiting because the door was tossed the wrong way and became an obstruction.

The exits illustrated above are "Type III," usually found over the wings. The FAA requires that opening any exit should be "simple, obvious and not require exceptional effort." But passengers in actual evacuations were often confused and ineffective, and most admitted to not reading the instructions. This led to a change in procedures; today you must be "qualified" if you sit next to an exit, that is, willing and able to open the door. A flight attendant will probably query you before take-off.

In the event of an evacuation, the largest doors, the one's used for boarding, will most likely be opened by a flight crew member. The reason is, there are usually crew members in the forward and aft ends of the airplane. But overwing exits, like the ones shown above, will most likely be opened by passengers because they will get there first.

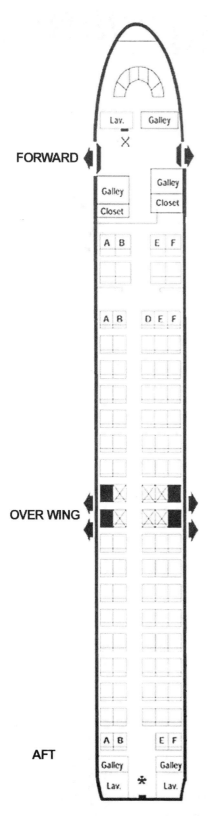

A good example of why you should carefully observe where the emergency exits are located. This Fokker 100 meets safety requirements for evacuation with both Forward and Over Wing emergency exits.

Note, however, there are no exits in the aft section of the airplane. A passenger may intuitively head in that direction because many aircraft do have exits in the rear.

Another factor is that flight attendants are usually posted near emergency exits, to assist passengers and open doors as quickly as possible. Note the "X" up front (near the word "Forward") which is the jumpseat for the flight attendant. This is a good location.

But note the asterisk (*) in the Aft section, the other position for a flight attendant. The distance between Aft to Over Wing sections, says the National Transportation Safety Board, may be too great a distance (24 feet) for the flight attendant to reach the Over Wing area. The Board recommended that the flight attendant position be moved to the door location.

A wise passenger, after sitting down, observes the location of the nearest exit.

Chapter 9

Cabin Decompression

For comfortable breathing without an oxygen mask, your airliner draws in thin air at high altitude and compresses it for the cabin. Although a few hardy souls have climbed Mt. Everest (29,000 feet) without oxygen, pressure in an airplane usually holds "cabin altitude" at a reasonable 8,000 feet or so.

Losing Air

Cabin pressure can drop several ways. A leaking door seal may allow air to escape, a window may shatter or bullets are fired in an attack. If the leak is slow, the airplane pressurization system can keep up with it and passengers won't notice a difference. Rapid decompression, however, is serious because it is life-threatening. (It is generally believed that bullet holes will not cause catastrophic loss of pressure.)

As anyone who's flown on an airplane may know, oxygen masks drop down in the event of depressurization. It happens automatically when cabin altitude is sensed at about 14,000 feet. For several thousand feet above that you may remain conscious and actually feel good (euphoria). Much above that, however, is fatal.

The effect of depressurization is that high-pressure air in the cabin rushes outside, where the pressure is lower. Fog may appear in the cabin as temperature drops. If the opening is large, decompression may be explosive---and carry objects outside. During a flight of a B-747 near Hawaii, a cargo door blew out, taking a large section of the fuselage with it. Nine passengers were lost.

Another decompression occurred when one-third of the roof of a B-737 blew off in flight. Only one life was lost; a person walking through the cabin

Life Insurance in Your Lap

A seat belt can save your life in a catastrophic decompression. People are urged to remain belted to avoid injury in turbulent air, but decompression is another good reason. Because it is extremely rare, decompression is more likely to hurt an eardrum because air trapped in the body tries to push out.

As soon as low pressure is sensed in the cabin, the oxygen mask drops down and dangles in front of you. If it doesn't appear reach out and pull a free one from another seat.

Flight attendants report cases of passengers warned of a slow decompression but who fail to take it seriously. They don't don the oxygen mask and often suffer severe hypoxia.

Get It Flowing

When your mask appears, be aware that it is not delivering oxygen. As the flight attendant demonstrated during the cabin briefing, tug on the mask to get oxygen flowing. Don't expect the bag to inflate and collapse as you breathe, like it does in a TV hospital drama. And if you are tending to a child, don your mask first to keep your senses sharp.

If the decompression is serious the pilots make an emergency descent to get the airplane below 10,000 feet as quickly as possible. Speed brakes deployed from the wings may cause bumpiness in flight. When the airplane levels out, the cabin crew will issue further instructions because you may be in a mountainous area. The crew might carry portable oxygen bottles if the airplane needs to fly above 10,000 ft to clear obstacles.

Chapter 10

Ditching: The Water Landing

Touching down on the water while the airplane is under control of the pilots is known as "ditching". The odds against it are astronomical; for 50 years following World War II, no commercial transport flying the North Atlantic ditched in deep-water ocean. That's reassuring when you consider that at any one time there are about 200 airliners flying that route. A major reason is the jet engine. It's about ten times more reliable than the old piston type.

Are More Engines Safer?

International flights were once flown only by airplanes with four engines, joined later by 3-engine aircraft, such as the L-1011, DC-10 and MD-11. Today, the mid-size 2-engine transport---B-767, B-777---is taking over those routes. Despite fewer engines, these aircraft have proven remarkably trouble-free. The old wisdom was the more engines, the safer the airplane---but that has faded from public perception.

Before you board an overseas flight, you may see the letters "ETOPS" painted on the side of the airplane. It means "Extended Range Twin-Engine Operations". Without this certification, an airliner with two engines may not go over water more than 60 minutes' flying time from an airport it can land on. But if the aircraft meets higher standards of maintenance, reliability and training, it can extend that to 180 minutes. By the year 2000, the rule extended to 207 minutes, allowing twins to fly the Pacific, notably the 2600 miles from California to Hawaii. An ETOPS rating widens the pilots' choice of shorter, fuel-saving routes over open ocean.

Old-time 4-engine pilots cast a fishy eye at ETOPS. They spell out ETOPS as, "Engines Turn or Passengers Swim".

Then there's the infamous "Bermuda Triangle". It should be renamed the "Bermuda Angel".   Hundreds of books, movies and TV shows ignore the fact that the Bermuda Triangle lies across the most heavily traveled air route in the world. There hasn't been an airline ditching there for half a century.

There have been two close calls, though.   During 2001, a twin-engine Airbus over the mid-Atlantic with 291 passengers aboard had a double-engine failure. In an extraordinary feat of airmanship, the pilots glided to an airport in the Azores 81 miles away and landed safely. The trouble turned out to be a mechanical problem in the fuel system. So, despite an almost unblemished record of oceanic flying by the airlines, the possibility of ditching lurks in the background.

The loss of one, or even all, engines on an airliner does not mean a quick plunge to the sea. Even the heaviest craft has a "glide ratio"; for every thousand feet high, it can glide forward more than a mile. During the descent, pilots operate the flight controls and attempt a survivable landing (as happened in the Airbus mentioned above). NASA's Space Shuttle, in fact, does every landing that way. Once the Shuttle lowers into the atmosphere, all engine power is spent. Yet the astronauts glide it to a gentle touchdown by maneuvering the flight controls.

Seaworthiness

Federal regulations require that any airline carrying passengers more than 50 miles from land must do a demonstration ditching. A real airplane is often used but an actual water landing is not required. When the airplane was designed, the airplane manufacturer had to assure that all emergency exits in a ditching will remain above the waterline when the airplane comes to rest. During the demo, darkness, blocked exits and fire are simulated. The crew must move over 500 passengers out in less than 90 seconds.

In a real ditching, the airplane is usually in flight when passengers and crew are instructed to put on life preservers, remove life rafts from storage and inflate rafts or slides. It must be accomplished within six minutes. When pilots want flight attendants to start the procedure, they might announce "Easy Victor," phonetics for EV, meaning "Evacuate". Other airlines might use a loud horn, while some announce "Evacuate".

After the ditching, when everyone emerges and boards life rafts, a crewmember describes how to use each piece of emergency equipment, such as radios and signal flares. Be ready for the possibility of being called on by the crew to help launch the life rafts.

Flight attendants are dedicated professionals who work heroically to shepherd you to safety. But ditching could be a terrifying experience that may not proceed according to the book. The more you understand the event, the greater your chances of surviving if you're on your own.

What Goes Wrong

The most appalling statistic on ditching is that most fatalities are caused by *drowning* after the airplane is on the surface. Death is not caused by crash impact, toxic gases or structural failure, but an inability of the person to remain afloat. This emphasizes your responsibility to know how to don the life jacket, locate and understand emergency exits, use the slide and board the raft.

In short-range aircraft (which may fly an hour offshore) your seat cushion may serve as flotation. In small airliners there may be no slide at the overwing exit. Long-range aircraft often have slides which convert to rafts. This information is available in the briefing and safety cards.

You will be instructed not to inflate your life jacket while inside the airplane because it may obstruct your passage. Flight attendants will show where to exit and how to board the raft. If you're in the water at night, be aware that life rafts have ropes along the sides for gripping and can be boarded at both ends.

An evacuation slide, like the one shown at the left, can detach and become a raft (right). In some airplanes, the life raft is stowed separately in a ceiling compartment near the door. The instructions tell what to do if a life raft doesn't inflate automatically. Some require manual operation of a lever, others have a manual back-up if the automatic feature doesn't function.

Basic Rules for Ditching

•Listen carefully to the oral briefing before take-off about a "water landing" and study the safety equipment described and pictured for your airplane.

•How fast you get out usually depends on the flight attendants. Follow their instructions. But if a crewmember is not there, you're on your own. Act quickly and decisively to get to the exit.

•If there is no life raft, stay together in the water. Group together for warmth.

•Rescuers advise: "Do not give up."

In the Water

When your whole body is immersed in water, there is risk of hypothermia, even when the water is not frigid. To discover ways to improve survival, especially for injured persons and children, the problem was investigated by the FAA's Civil Aeromedical Institute. It assumed there was no time to don life jackets and the sole flotation was the seat cushion. After simulating trials in a pool, they drew several conclusions. First, passengers in the water must remain close together to prevent anyone from drifting away and getting lost. People in groups are also more conspicuous to rescuers. By huddling together, you suffer less shock and hypothermia and gain a better sense of well-being.

From their tests in the water, FAA researchers devised several techniques. Two people should face each other and hold their flotation cushions between them, each grasping the straps of the other. If a third person has no seat cushion or is injured, he or she should be held between the cushions of the two people. A group should form a cluster by grasping arms. They should interlock ankles or legs to stabilize the group and conserve body heat. The illustrations show several recommended positions.

Remember, though, this was a worst-case scenario. In most instances of ditching, you will board a raft and avoid immersion in the water.

Chances for Rescue

If a ditching occurs near land, help may be on the way in minutes. The crew is in instant contact with Air Traffic Control and radar is tracking your position. A thousand miles offshore, rescue takes longer. A ditching, however, is not like most airplane accidents, which happen with little warning. An airplane crossing the ocean is at high altitude, giving regular position reports and taking more than 10 minutes to reach the surface after total engine failure.

One Engine Out

Let's assume your flight is cruising above 30,000 feet when the crew is warned of problems in one engine. To prevent unleashing destructive forces, the captain may elect to shut it down. He begins

In tests conducted by the Civil Aviation Authority of Great Britain, reseachers learned important survival techniques at sea. If you are not in a life raft and the water is cold, it is most essential to conserve body heat. The cold may cause you to lose the use of your hands so if there's more than one person, quickly group together. Huddle with the sides of your chests and lower bodies pressed together. If there are children, sandwich them in the middle of the group.

Don't attempt to swim to shore unless you are a strong swimmer and the distance is small, say, less than about a half-mile.

If rescuers arrive on the scene, follow their instructions explicitly. Don't grab for cables or do things on your own initiative; the rescuers will give you instructions.

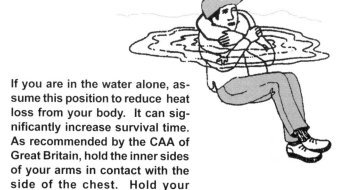

If you are in the water alone, assume this position to reduce heat loss from your body. It can significantly increase survival time. As recommended by the CAA of Great Britain, hold the inner sides of your arms in contact with the side of the chest. Hold your thighs together and raise them slightly to protect the groin region.

a descent to lower altitude to thicker air, where the remaining engine can sustain level flight. He radios Air Traffic Control and describes the problem. As the airplane cruises along, with passengers unaware, the captain declares an emergency to ATC. The controller immediately gives the captain priority treatment to assure best communications, routing and clearance from other traffic.

In nearly all cases of an engine shutdown, the result is a safe landing. Jet aircraft fly remarkably well on one engine and pilots practice it every six months in a flight simulator. The chance of losing the second powerplant are vanishingly small, but everyone must be prepared.

If you're flying on one engine in a real situation, ATC will offer to send rescue aircraft to escort your airplane. The controller tells the captain the location of ships in the area and briefs him on the weather and condition of the sea, especially wind direction, and how the swells are moving. These are crucial to a successful water landing. If the wind is strong at the surface and the sea is calm, he will probably land directly into the wind which slows the airplane for the softest contact. But if ocean swells are high, he may touch down parallel to the waves to avoid striking them head on.

Not all ditching alarms end in a watery landing. In 1999, an international flight took off from San Francisco and headed for London. Three hours later, passengers were horrified when the PA system ordered them to put on their life jackets and prepare for ditching at sea. The warning sounded a second time, spreading more anxiety through the cabin---until flight attendants discovered the reason. Someone had mistakenly pressed a button activating the recorded ditching message. The airline apologized profusely (but speculated that a passenger had unwittingly pressed the button).

Chapter 11

Comfort and Safety in the Cabin

Will I get Sick in an Airplane?

Many passengers and crew members complain about stagnant air, thirst and discomfort such as red and itchy eyes.

"Will I catch the flu?" they ask when another passenger sneezes.

"What was the funny smell in the cabin during take-off?"

"It's too cold…too hot…too stuffy."

Passengers are also concerned about the spread of disease in flight, particularly during reduced air-conditioning operation and lower air exchange. After a study in 1998, the American Medical Association concluded that under usual aircraft procedures, cabin air quality *does not* represent a significant risk for transmission of infectious diseases. Passengers and crew should remember that infection is an everyday risk, but lower on an airplane due to the constant exchange of cabin air. I have no empirical evidence, but I think risk of infection is probably greater in elevators, stores and offices.

Drinking Liquids

I've discovered no magic bullet, but a number of steps may make you feel better after a long flight. Jet lag is less debilitating when you drink fluids during the trip and do not drink excessive diuretics, such as coffee. I regularly dampen my nasal passages with water, breathing through a wet towel a few minutes every few hours. The amount of hydrating fluid on a long flight depends on the person, but one doctor advised me that if you need to urinate every couple of hours, your hydration level is probably adequate. Some people recommend immersing your body in water, such as a bath or pool, after a long flight.

Air Quality

Contaminants in cabin air, such as ozone, burned and unburned gases, toxic aerosols, engine oil, hydraulic fluid and deicing fluid have attracted attention over recent years. In normal aircraft operations, however, air quality in the cabin is usually as safe, if not safer, than air in many large cities. One benefit of the inflight cabin over city air: cabin air is changed every two to six minutes.

If there is a malfunction in the aircraft, and noxious fumes reach the air-conditioning system, cabin air could have severe effects on passengers and crew. Thankfully, these occasions are rare. If you experience one, place a cloth over your face and keep your eyes closed. Quick reaction by the pilots should isolate the cause. They have various methods to increase cabin air exchange to offset the adverse condition.

Some people believe airlines expose their customers to an unhealthy environment for the sake of profits. This is illogical, to say the least. Airline companies rely on repeat customers for their existence and can't afford to alienate them . Within the confines of economic viability, airlines make every effort to ensure a comfortable trip. The bottom line is that passengers and airline crew must ride in an air-conditioned cabin to travel rapidly from one point to another.

Jet Lag

Passengers may worry whether the crew flying the airplane is alert because the media has published articles on pilots falling asleep on the job. While any pilot who flies over several time zones may become fatigued, pilots on international routes suffer the most. Hold on to your seats, folks…but experts say that pilots should be encouraged to take a nap at the wheel--- but under carefully controlled conditions.

Twenty million Americans perform shift work and suffer major disruptions in their body physiology, social activities and family life due to sleep loss and disturbed circadian (day-night) rhythms. Sleep is a complex state vital to survival. The average sleep needed per night is 8 hours---but as little as one hour less can cause sleepiness and degraded performance the next day. If continued over time, sleep debt accumulates. For passengers traveling intensively over long distances, fatigue can be very debilitating. For pilots, cumulative fatigue is downright dangerous.

Circadian Rhythm

Humans have a pacemaker in the base of the brain that regulates functions around the clock, for example; sleep/wake periods, body temperature, hormone secretion, digestion, performance and mood. Disturbing the daily circadian rhythm by crossing time zones can profoundly influence normal tasks---equally affecting crew and passengers.

Technology may leap ahead, but humans are still central to aviation, which operates 24 hours a day. Flight crews and frequent flyers who routinely cross oceans or continents, therefore, are more prone to physiological effects.

A study by NASA reveals interesting data on fatigue in pilots. The subjects were 29 males with an average age of 52, flying Boeing-747 aircraft on four international patterns.

• Spontaneous sleep episodes, lasting from microseconds to minutes, occur when a pilot is very fatigued. Extremely fatigued pilots can literally fall asleep with their eyes open.

• Recuperation from sleep debt requires approximately 8 hours of deep sleep over one or two nights.

• Sleeping during periods contrary to normal circadian cycles is shorter and not as deep.

• Sleep outside a pilot's time zone is more effective if part of it falls within the pilot's normal circadian rhythm.

• Frequent disruption to the circadian rhythm can lead to being chronically out of step with local time because body functions adapt at different rates. Unless a pilot is given sufficient time to recover at home after a multi-day pattern, he or she will exist in a state of flux.

• Adapting to a new time zone takes longer when more time zones are crossed. It also takes longer after eastward, as opposed to westward flight.

• Two periods of maximum sleepiness occur in a 24-hour circadian cycle; 3 to 5 a.m. and 3 to 5 p.m. If you have not adapted to local time in a new destination, expect to feel tired at odd times of the day.

• The intensity of Circadian rhythm reduces with age; older pilots have more difficulty adapting to circadian disruptions.

• Older pilots (50-60) reported significantly greater sleep loss per day than younger pilots (30-40).

• Morning-type pilots have greater difficulty adapting to time change than night-types. Older pilots tend to be morning type.

• Extroverted pilots adapt more readily to time-zone shifts.

• Alcohol and caffeine seriously degrade quality of sleep.

Sleep Deficit

I conducted a simple study of my own to evaluate sleep loss for a typical long-haul pilot. The subject ---I'll call him Joe---was a B-747 pilot flying for an international airline. Joe operated a typical pattern; departing Los Angeles, crossing the Pacific Ocean four times, and returning to Los Angeles on the sixth day. Joe is middle-aged, married, physically fit and conscientious about his health.

Because of regulations about duty time, the flight from Los Angeles to Narita, Japan carried a "heavy" crew (two captains, one first officer and two flight engineers). On this leg Joe enjoyed a 3-hour inflight crew rest. All other flights during the pattern were single crew: captain, first officer and flight engineer.

During the five days away from Los Angeles, there was one normal sleep period. This was during a Vancouver lay-over coinciding with Pacific Standard Time; Joe's circadian rhythm had not deviated from this time zone since his departure from Los Angeles.

With exception of the period mentioned above, Joe's sleep was sporadic, and shorter than when at home in Los Angeles. In the five days since leaving home Joe got 26.25 hours of sleep, as opposed to a recommended 40 hours. That was an average of 5.25 hours per day.

His sleep deficit occurred in two stages: In the first two days, Joe accumulated 6 hours of sleep loss. According to the NASA study, Joe might have recovered in Vancouver, where he experienced normal 8-hour sleep. He was fully recovered before operating his flight back to Narita.

The second stage of sleep deficit---the last two days of the pattern---he accumulated 7.75 hours of sleep loss. The most probable time for Joe to experience degraded performance would be at maximum sleep deprivation---with such problems as attention loss, spontaneous sleep or other incapacitation. They might occur during landing in Vancouver on the third day of the pattern, and the final landing into Los Angeles on the sixth day. More disturbing is that Joe had only 3 hours of sleep in 29 hours before landing in Los Angeles. The result of my study indicated that the final landing in Los Angeles---one of the country's busiest airports---could be the most affected.

Fatigue

NASA's Fatigue Countermeasure Program identified four factors to be examined when crew fatigue is suspected in an incident or accident. They are: acute sleep loss and cumulative sleep debt, continuous hours of wakefulness, time of day and circadian rhythm effects, and sleep disorders. NASA's Aviation Safety Reporting System indicates that approximately 21% of reported aviation incidents are related to fatigue.

A study performed by NASA and the FAA demonstrated that long-haul pilot vigilance and performance can be enhanced by *planning short sleep opportunities during flight*. Positive effects were demonstrated by crew members who took 30-40 minute naps on the flight deck. They maintained good performance at the end of their flight. The short nap had acted as an acute inflight safety valve.

Despite the evidence, the FAA does not sanction inflight naps while pilots are on duty. This could be for several reasons. Some air routes are busier than others, for example; a flight across the Pacific has long periods between (radio) reporting points, whereas a flight across Russian airspace requires frequent voice contact with controllers.

Another reason could be that in a three-man crew, if one pilot takes a nap, two crew members remain vigilant. This provides a cross-check where errors are less likely. In a two-man cockpit that safety factor is missing. The general public---speaking through the media---has expressed outrage that pilots may actually asleep on the job.

I believe guidelines are needed to encourage *all* long-haul crew members to take refreshing inflight naps when conditions permit. The alternative, especially in a two-man cockpit, is de-graded performance and lower safety margins. The public and the FAA need to change their attitude and insist that pilots be autho-rized to invigorate themselves this way before landing. Passen-gers, of course, should catch a nap, too--- even if the flight is only 4 hours.

International flights will always require pilots to operate long hours across time zones. Because human physiology is difficult to change, airlines need to be aware of pilot limitations and formu-late rosters to maximize rest. While the bottom line is important in the hypercompetitive, international airline industry, nobody is served by an accident caused by tired pilots.

Fighting Fatigue

From many years of long-haul experience, I have found ways to reduce the problem. First, minimize loss by getting ample sleep whenever you're home. When you travel, take advantage of any time you feel sleepy regardless of local time. Any sleep is benefi-cial in reducing a sleep debt. If this means you will be up in the middle of the night, have a snack and reading material at hand to keep you occupied.

Exercise may enhance deep sleep, but avoid strenuous exercise within 6 hours of going to bed. Heavy exercise stimulates physiological activity and interferes with sleep. Avoid caffeine for at least 3 hours before bedtime; however, during flight, the stimulating effects of caffeine can be used in moderation to keep alert---especially for pilots. Be aware that caffeine is a diuretic and too much causes dehydration. It can also cause shakiness. Avoid alcohol, also a diuretic. Limit the amount you eat and try not to salt your food to reduce stomach bloating and dehydration.

Your body takes several days to adapt its circadian rhythm to a new location. Don't expect to fall into a normal sleep pattern overnight. Ease into the transition by catching an afternoon nap. But make sure to set the alarm. Because your nap may fall in a period when your body is accustomed to being asleep at night, you may wake 4 or 5 hours later. Get to bed a little later each day, before reaching the point of exhaustion, so that over 3 or 4 days you will adapt to local time.

Your Portable Electronics

Any time electricity passes through a wire, it may radiate interference harmful to aircraft radio and other electronics. Avionics on the aircraft are tested for electrical emission and compatibility. Where interference is excessive, wires and cabinets are shielded to contain it. Shielding, however, is heavy and expensive aboard an aircraft.

As any travelling person knows, airlines have strict rules on passenger use of electronic devices. There is evidence that some portable electronic devices (PED) can interfere with aircraft systems. In the 1960's an airline reported that a navigation system indicated 10 degrees off whenever a passenger operated an FM radio. Airline reports fell into three categories:

1. Where the PED is suspected of causing a problem when it switched on.

2. When the problem went away when the PED was switched off.

3. Strong correlation between the problem and PED use.

That is, the problem started when the PED was switched on and went away when it was off again.

Only a few events over the years show a strong correlation. Boeing conducted exhaustive tests, on one occasion buying the actual PED from the passenger to test it in flight on the same airplane. In every lab and flight test no case was duplicated. Boeing did determine that some devices emit stronger radio signals than others and the possibility exists for airplane systems to be affected in certain circumstances.

Types of Passenger Electronic Devices

PEDs are either intentional or non-intentional transmitters of radio signals. Intentional transmitters include cell phones and pagers. The non-intentional PED doesn't transmit signals in its normal operation, but may emit interference. These include CD players, laptop computers and electronic games.

Although unable to replicate interference in the lab or on flight tests, authorities concluded that enough anecdotal evidence exists to limit their use. In the guidelines that followed, airlines allow passengers to use a PED on the ground until the time the cabin door closes. This is when pilots start engines and taxi for takeoff. The transmitting PED must not be used until the airplane is again on the ground and parked at the arrival gate, with the cabin door open.

After takeoff---usually indicated by a signal from the cockpit---the majority of airlines allow passengers to turn on non-transmitting PEDs. They must be turned off before the airplane descends for landing.

A problem I witness with cell phones is passengers' reticence to switch them off until the last minute. It is not unusual to taxi for takeoff and hear several cell phones begin ringing. It is unlikely to cause a problem (experts put the odds at about 1 in one million), but passengers must follow rules that, after all, ensure their safety. As Dr. Laura says on her radio show, "Now, go and do the right thing."

Vibrations and Noises in Flight

A jetliner is a complex machine that literally reshapes itself during flight. Swept-wing aircraft---and this includes most commercial airliners---operate at high altitude and high speed. Engineers design the wings to be most efficient during cruise, the longest phase of flight. On takeoff and landing, however, when the aircraft flies at low speed, the high-speed wings cannot generate sufficient lift. Various devices such as flaps, therefore, move out to increase the wing area and change its curvature. This increases lift needed at the low speeds of take off and landing.

There is also movement in other control surfaces, often visible from cabin windows; ailerons, spoilers and speed brakes. Ailerons are moveable panels along the wing's trailing edge. They move together with spoilers---flat panels stowed on top of the wing. If the pilot turns the aircraft to the left, the aileron of the left wing moves up, as the right wing aileron moves down. This causes the airplane to roll to the left. At the same time, a spoiler panel on the left wing moves up. This helps to move the left wing down, especially at low air speed.

During approach to an airport, Air Traffic Control instructs pilots to slow down or rapidly descend to lower altitude. Now the speed brakes are extended, panels which rise from the upper surface of the wing. Raising speed brakes reduces lift across the wing and increases drag, thus reducing aircraft speed and increasing rate of descent. Speed brakes are usually extended for a minute or two while pilots adjust the airplane's speed and altitude to ATC's request. When these panels are extended, passengers will notice vibration and noise. This is buffeting, a disruption of air flowing across the wing. The intensity depends on the aircraft's speed and altitude.

Let's take a look at other noises and vibrations during a normal flight.

Engine start

During pushback from the gate and engine starting, passengers may notice a small disruption in the flow of cabin air. At this time the air conditioning system is briefly redirected to help start the engines. Engines take approximately 30 seconds to start, but pilots may leave one engine shut down to save fuel if they anticipate a long taxi for takeoff or delay in ATC clearance. A low-level whine sounds as the engines start, gradually increasing and levelling off when the engine reaches idle speed. From that point, when the pilot increases power, noise increases proportionally. The loudness depends on the passenger's seat location and whether the engines are mounted under the wing or at the rear of the fuselage.

Taxi

Now the pilots are extending flaps and testing flight controls for freedom of movement. Whirring or whining sounds are heard as hydraulic motors drive the flaps to takeoff position. Don't be concerned if control surfaces seem to be moving this way and that; they are testing every flight control thoroughly before takeoff. During this time you may hear an engine running down. It's actually an auxiliary power unit, often located near the wheel well, being shut down before takeoff. There may be changes in airflow into the cabin as air conditioning packs are switched on. They have air-driven turbines that might be audible in the passenger cabin.

Takeoff

The pilots may either stop on the runway before applying takeoff power or turn immediately onto the runway for a rolling takeoff. When takeoff clearance is received, they push each engine up a little and check for normal indications. Full takeoff power is then applied, engines emitting maximum sound.

As the airplane accelerates down the runway you are forced into the back of the seat. Sometimes a takeoff roll is so bumpy it seems as if the airplane must have blown a tire. The bumpiness mostly happens on cold winter mornings after the airplane sat overnight, causing flat spots on the tires. In about ten minutes of taxi time the tires to warm up and the flat spots disappear.

Another cause of a bumpy takeoff roll is when the aircraft runs exactly down the center of the runway. Lighting fixtures located on the center line protrude slightly above the surface and bump the nose wheel as the airplane accelerates.

As the airplane rotates (the nose rises), its climb angle is determined by its gross weight, traffic in the area and weather. For most jetliners, the climb angle is around 11 to 16 degrees. When the pilot recognizes positive rate of climb in the instruments, he or she retracts the landing gear. In about 10 seconds, hydraulic actuators operate gear doors, retract the landing gear trucks and close the doors. Noises and bumps are audible at this time.

As the airplane accelerates, the flaps are retracted, accompanied by whining sounds of hydraulic motors. ATC tells the pilots a route to fly away from the airport and the speed to maintain for the climb. Since there may be inbound and outbound traffic, ATC may request your airplane to hold a certain altitude. If this happens, the pilots may pull power off significantly and change the airplane's attitude. There is a reduction in engine noise, so there's no cause for alarm. When ATC re-clears the pilots to climb, power is added and the attitude increases again.

When the airplane reaches approximately 10,000 feet, and conditions permit, fasten-seat-belt signs are switched off. You are now free to move about and go to the lavatory, but this is also an indication to flight attendants they may prepare for inflight service.

Cruise

As the airplane burns fuel, it loses weight. Depending on weather and ATC approval, pilots climb to higher altitudes at various stages of the flight. If they encounter turbulence or adverse winds that lower fuel efficiency, they may descend to a lower altitude. Astute passengers notice slight changes in engine noise, attitude or pressure, but the effects are negligible. At the end of cruise, engine power is reduced to idle to begin the descent.

Descent

Since cabin pressure is maintained at an altitude of 6,000 to 8,000 feet during cruise, pressure is gradually increased during descent. On your arrival on the ground, it should equal the pressure at the airport. Pressurization is automatic but can be fine-tuned by pilots. They adjust for smooth changes, but it is normal to feel differences in your ears during descent. If pressure builds in your inner ear, pinch your nostrils and blow gently. This helps to open the Eustachian tubes and equalize the pressure difference.

As the airplane approaches the airport, ATC issues speeds and courses to slot you into arrival traffic. Speed brakes may be deployed to comply with ATC instructions. Flaps extend in stages as the airplane slows to its final approach speed of around 140 knots. The actual speed is affected by the airplane's weight and prevailing weather.

Landing

Pilots pride themselves in smooth landings, but there are so many dynamic factors in touching down that a bump may be felt. Once the wheels are on the ground, speed brakes deploy to reduce lift. This shifts the airplane's weight to the wheels for effective braking. Most jetliner brakes apply automatically and modulate the deceleration. Reverse thrust is also applied to the engines to further slow the airplane's momentum.

The airplane engines are not actually reversed. Sleeves or blocker doors on the engine are programmed to deploy by the pilot's actions. They redirect the engine's thrust to slow the airplane when reverse thrust is selected. In other words, the engine turns the same way, but its output is turned around to stop, rather than accelerate, the airplane.

During taxi to the gate, flaps are retracted, speed brakes stowed and the auxiliary power unit started. Passengers should keep seat belts fastened because there may be sudden stops during taxi.

Dangerous Goods

Explosive or flammable goods are considered dangerous. The category includes goods that can injure a person or do damage to the aircraft. Each country's aviation authority has its own rules, but ICAO sets the international standard.

Since September 11, passenger baggage was severely limited. Carry-on luggage is restricted to one bag that will fit into the overhead bin or under a seat, plus a small briefcase, handbag or portfolio. It's the flight attendants' responsibility to check that luggage is stowed correctly so passengers are not blocked during an emergency evacuation.

Hazardous materials must be declared. The fines are heavy in the U.S. for violating regulations that apply to airlines, express package carriers, or U.S. Postal Service. If convicted, violators can be penalized up to $27,500 per occurrence, criminal penalties of up to $500,000 and up to 5 years' imprisonment.

Under certain conditions, unloaded firearms and radioactive pharmaceuticals may be carried in the cargo hold after packing them according to stringent regulations. But definitely check with the airline before transporting any item you have doubts about.

The following devices, many also prohibited in checked luggage, are restricted by the FAA in airplanes:

• Knives of any length, type or composition.

• Any cutting or impaling device whatsoever, including razor blades, box cutters, ice picks, knitting needles, scissors, corkscrews, and nail files. Some screeners even confiscate nail clippers.

• Other weapons, such as throwing stars, swords or other martial arts devices commonly used in competitions.

• Baseball and softball bats, pool cues, ski poles, hockey sticks or other device that could be used as a club.

• Explosives, firearms, strike-anywhere matches, fireworks, flares, gunpowder, ammunition, blasting caps, dynamite.

• Flammable liquids or solids, such as gasoline, propane, butane, flammable paints, paint thinners, solvents, some adhesives, cigarette lighter fuel and refills containing unabsorbed liquid fuel (other than liquefied gas), and flammable perfumes (in large quantities). Some hazardous liquids or gases may be carried onboard if each container is less than 16 fluid ounces (473 ml) and the total is less than 70 fluid ounces (2.07 lts). However, other flammable liquids, such as 100-proof alcohol, are banned from cabin stowage; if you have any doubt, check with airline before boarding.

• Flammable aerosol containers, such as hair spray, canned spray paint, insect repellent, carbon dioxide cartridges, oxygen tanks (other than required by passengers), chemical oxygen generators (used or unused), mace, tear gas, pepper spray, self-inflating rafts and refrigerated gases such as freon or liquid nitrogen.

• Oxidizers or organic peroxides, such as bleach, nitric acid, fertilizers, swimming pool or spa chemicals (chlorine), fiberglass repair kits.

• Poisons, such as weed killers, pesticides, insecticides, rodent poisons, arsenic and cyanides.

• Infectious materials, such as medical laboratory specimens, viral organisms, bacterial cultures.

• Corrosives, such as drain cleaners, car batteries, wet cell batteries, acids, alkalis, lye, mercury. If you have an electric wheel chair, it must be carried in accordance with airline regulations. The battery will be disconnected, removed from the chair and its terminals insulated against possible short circuits.

• Organics, such as fiberglass resins, peroxides.

• Radioactive materials, radioactive pharmaceuticals or isotopes. The items may be carried in the cargo hold after strict packing regulations are applied.

•Dry ice in excess of 4 pounds (1.8 kg) is restricted, but lesser quantities may be carried with packed perishables providing the package is vented. Dry ice gives off carbon dioxide gas as it evaporates.

• Magnetic materials, such as loudspeakers and laboratory equipment. These may interfere with the compass in the airplane.

Personal items

There are exceptions to hazardous goods for personal use, but this usually means small quantities. For example, flammable perfumes are allowed, but only less than 70 fluid ounces (each container must be less than 10 fluid ounces). Normal matches and liquid gas lighters may be carried on your person. Equipment for medical needs or to support handicapped passengers may be carried.

Customs

Rules against hazardous goods are uniform around the world, based on international agreement. But you can never be sure whether other countries have unique limitations. This is particularly true for customs laws. Japan restricted importing of Sudafed for years, a medication available over the counter in the United States. While to most Americans this would seem extreme, Japanese customs often asked passengers whether they were carrying this medication. This is a good example of not applying your country's laws when traveling. Many items that seem harmless, such as plant seeds, are also banned in most countries. I once had microwave popcorn confiscated by an Australian customs agent; he felt the product fell under his country's ban on importing seeds.

The best advice is to declare any concerns to airline staff before departure. If you are traveling to another country, read the customs forms closely to avoid a possible fine. If there is any doubt, declare the item on arrival. The worst that can then happen is the item will be confiscated. Custom officers in all countries take their job seriously and do not suffer fools lightly.

The best example I can think of for complying with prohibitions on dangerous goods is the ValuJet crash in the Florida Everglades. This tragic accident in 1966 took the lives of 110 passengers and crew. The NTSB found the most probable cause was intense fire in the forward cargo compartment that burned through control cables. ValuJet had been carrying more than 100 expired chemical oxygen generators, incorrectly marked empty, and not protected with safety caps. The flight also carried three aircraft tires in the same compartment. On DC-9 aircraft, lower cargo holds were classified Class D compartments. This was assigned on the assumption that restricted airflow into the compartment would extinguish fire by oxygen starvation. In ValuJet's case, a ready supply of oxygen fed the fire that broke out approximately 6 minutes after takeoff. ValuJet had not been permitted to carry hazardous materials.

This demonstrates the perils of noncompliance, but even products in everyday home use may become hazardous in flight. Pressure and temperature variations cause leakage, generate noxious fumes or start fires. Business travelers with product samples must be vigilant to avoid taking harmful goods on a flight. People involved in hobbies or sports, and anyone carrying chemicals or dangerous substances are wise to check with the airline.

Dry Cabin

Airline passengers often complain about dry atmosphere in the cabin. Some are concerned that the low flow and recirculation of cabin air can increase infectious disease transmission. To allay these fears and see why the dry atmosphere is critical to safe operation of the airplane, consider these factors.

For many years aircraft manufacturers have fought water condensation inside the cabin. Air conditioning is provided by "bleed air" drawn from the engines, cooled, dehumidified and pressurized inside the cabin. At cruise altitude the skin of the aircraft cools rapidly. Insulation blankets just inside the skin prevent the cool temperature from reaching the cabin, but small gaps in the blankets inevitably develop and cabin air contacts the cold aircraft skin.

Most water is removed from the air before it passes into the cabin, but moisture is added by passenger breathing. Moist air in contact with the cold aircraft skin condenses and forms frost. When the aircraft descends, its skin temperature increases and the frost evaporates rapidly. The airplane is designed to drain the water overboard, but if gaps in the insulation are large enough, some water may drip into the cabin interior or infiltrate the blankets. This is why moisture may drip from your overhead area as the flight nears its destination.

Boeing studied the problem and found that condensation depends not only on cabin humidity, but on buoyancy rates. The buoyancy effect is the pressure difference behind and in front of the insulation. This difference is slightly negative near the ceiling and slightly positive near the floor. As a result, most frost forms near the crown of the cabin.

Several factors increase moisture, for example; a high passenger load increases moisture from breathing, high airplane utilization keeps the airplane longer at low temperature, low cruise speed, low cabin airflow and higher altitudes. Thus, the most severe moisture problems occur on aircraft with high-density seating, high loads and high utilization. Interestingly, outside atmospheric humidity levels seem to have little influence.

Adverse Effects

Insulation blankets within the aircraft structure are typically fiber-glass batting covered with waterproof, nonmetallic Mylar. Water runs over the Mylar surface similar to rain draining over roof shingles. Moisture drains into bilge areas and escapes overboard. If there are gaps between blankets or if the blanket is damaged, water drips into the cabin or accumulates in the insulation blanket. If water drips on passengers it may cause a complaint, but if sensitive electrical components are exposed to water, it's more serious.

"Wet-arcing" has been cited as the cause of electrical problems. On one 737-300 the difference between existing and new insulation blankets was approximately 80 pounds. Water-logged blankets increase costs because they add weight and conduct heat away. Accumulated water exacerbates corrosion and decreases the life of the airframe. Some maintenance technicians wrung out insulation blankets to drain water, but this damages the fiber-glass beyond repair and decreases its insulation.

Solving the Problem

It is difficult to eliminate moisture from aircraft cabins. Based on testing, Boeing determined that the best way is routine maintenance to be sure there's a clear path overboard for water. Ventilation that directs cabin air to the crown space of the fuselage also reduces the problem. This is not the case, however, in aircraft equipped with overhead re-circulation fans. Nomex felt can be added to upper surfaces of stowage bins and other ceiling areas to absorb water before it enters the cabin. Water evaporates from the panels when there is airflow in the cabin.

One answer to the problem is the Zonal Drying System, which has a slowly turning rotor filled with silica gel (a drying agent). Cabin air is drawn in, dried and expelled into the cabin above the ceiling panels. This lowers the dew point of cabin air, preventing condensation from forming on the skin inside the fuselage. A portion of the cabin air is heated inside the dryer, passed over the silica gel to reabsorb moisture, and directed to the recirculation system.

But we are still left with a relatively dry atmosphere in the passenger cabin. Wouldn't it be nice if we could raise passenger comfort by humidifying this air without producing moisture inside the airframe?

Humans feel most comfortable when the humidity is about 50 percent, but aircraft environments never reach this level. Because passenger breathing adds moisture, humidity varies with seating density, and is highest in closely-packed economy sections and lowest in first class. Even in the densest charter flight, humidity rarely exceeds 15 percent. Complaints include dry throat, eye and skin irritation, respiratory tract problems and general malaise. In the Zonal Comfort System, air passes through a wet pad where moisture is picked up, thereby cooling and humidifying it. Water is drawn from spare capacity in the aircraft's potable water system, so extra water need not be loaded.

The humidifier increases moisture in the most affected areas of the cabin, namely, business and first class. Water consumption is approximately 6 to 7 liters per hour. A long-haul airplane, such as an MD-11 needs two humidifiers, with water consumption of 100 to 150 liters for a ten-hour flight.

The benefits of moister air in the cabin are better sleep, less risk of getting a cold, less throat or eye irritation and an increase in food quality and sense of taste. While some have been installed on European carriers, the Zonal Drying System is yet to make an impact on U.S. airlines. Part of the problem is cost, and the manufacturer has yet to establish an operational track record. In the future, these systems should prove cost-effective and installed by all airlines. Until that time, passengers will wonder why they get rained on during descent---while cabin humidity is below that of a desert.

Weather

Airlines need to move passengers in all types of adverse weather and they do a remarkably good job. Pilots never knowingly enter conditions that affect safe operation, but unexpected weather may be encountered. Let's take a look at conditions which may affect your flight.

Wind Shear

Where layers of air move in opposite directions they create "wind shear" at the dividing line. Most dangerous is low-level wind shear, where strong changes in wind occur below 2,000 feet. It is most often caused by the violent rush of air out of a thunderstorm, but also results from cold and warm fronts or wind around buildings or hills. Wind shear becomes serious if the pilot cannot speed up or slow down sufficiently to fly out of it. Fortunately, today's jetliners are fitted with wind shear warning systems that advise when to avoid these areas.

Many airports are also equipped with wind shear detection on the ground. They measure wind strength and direction at several points around the airport. When a computer sees a major difference among them, it issues a wind shear alert. The control tower then advises all aircraft in the area.

Turbulence

Unstable air in clouds, storms, jet streams, cold or warm fronts, mountain ranges or wake turbulence from other aircraft can cause turbulence. Unfortunately, pilots cannot always determine when it occurs, especially when turbulence happens in clear air. That's why flight crews advise passengers to keep seat belts fastened whenever seated.

Turbulence causes the most common non-fatal passenger injuries. Despite warnings on the PA, approximately 58 passengers each year are injured because their seat belt was not fastened. Between 1981 and 1997, there were 342 incidents of turbulence reported by major airlines. Three people were killed (at least two had not fastened their seat belt), 80 seriously injured (73 were not wearing seat belts) and 769 received minor injuries.

Turbulence is classified as light, moderate, severe or extreme. Pilots tell flight attendants to take their seats if moderate turbulence or worse is expected. While the FAA, NASA and aerospace companies have been developing turbulence detectors, none is available at this writing. Even when a system reaches the market, it is likely to deliver only a 30 to 60 second warning. I *strongly* recommend that you keep your seat belt fastened while seated. If you are in the aisle or lavatory, be aware of handholds to help you maintain balance if the airplane suddenly pitches or rolls. If you are standing in the cabin with a vacant seat nearby, sit down quickly and fasten the seat belt. You can return to your seat once the "fasten seat belt" signed is off.

The following incidents are typical: A flight from Singapore to Sydney with 252 passengers and crew encountered turbulence that dropped the airplane 300 feet. Twelve people, including a pregnant woman, were injured---one required surgery. None of the injured passengers was wearing a seat belt. In another flight, one passenger was killed and several crew injured when a B-747 encountered severe turbulence over the Pacific Ocean two hours out of Japan. Much suffering can be avoided by treating the seat belt as crucial to your safety.

Clear Air Turbulence

After years of research on CAT---Clear Air Turbulence---practical systems are still not available. CAT cannot be detected by weather radar and strikes without warning. It usually occurs at high altitudes from effects of the jet stream, mountain waves and other phenomena that cause wind shear aloft. Air traffic controllers relay reports of CAT encounters among pilots but conditions shift quickly and may occur over a local area.

CAT is insidious because it catches passengers unaware. Sudden changes in altitude or attitude cause G-forces that lift you off your seat or slam you to the floor. In one encounter, a flight attendant hit her head on the ceiling, then was slammed to the floor so hard she received fatal neck injuries. For passengers, the seat belt firmly fastened is the first line of defense.

Wake Turbulence

When an airplane wing generates lift, it also throws off twisting masses of air from the wing tips. Called "vortices," they last several minutes, spread downward and outward from the flight path, and drift with the wind. Their strength and impact on other aircraft depend on the aircraft's weight, so wake turbulence is most important when following large jetliners.

Wake turbulence typically occurs in the vicinity of the airport. This is particularly true at airports that use parallel runways for takeoff and landing (which keeps arriving and departing flights closer).

In recent years commercial jets have been allowed to cruise at reduced separation (down to 1,000 feet vertically on some high altitude routes). This has the advantage of putting more aircraft in a limited airspace, but wake turbulence has been reported at higher altitudes.

Large jetliners encountering wake turbulence usually feel little more than light to moderate turbulence. On the other hand, small aircraft may suffer extreme up and down drafts, so they must take special precaution when following a heavy aircraft, in the air or on the ground. What makes pilots recognize wake turbulence is the short duration and the knowledge that another jetliner crossed their path.

Air traffic controllers space out all aircraft to minimize wake turbulence encounters, especially for landing and take off. Given the demands at large airports, however, these encounters occur from time to time. But the turbulence is usually short-lived and minor. I have been on dozens of flights through wake turbulence. Just keep in mind that encounters happen around airports, so maintain a policy of keeping your seat belt fastened around your hips.

Traveling With Kids

Children under two years can be carried on your lap when you travel, but the FAA recommends some form of restraint. Most people do not buy children of this age their own seat. They hope the plane will not be full and the child will get a seat anyway.

For your comfort and the safety of your child, consider purchasing a child seat. This is the only way to be sure your child can use a safety seat. The FAA recommends securing children under 20 pounds in a rear-facing child safety seat, and to place kids between 20 and 40 pounds in a forward-facing seat. There is about a 16-inch width in coach seats to accommodate your child's safety needs. It is best to place the child in the window or middle seat. You will need to bring your own child safety seat---airlines do not supply them.

Identify the exits closest to your seat and instruct your child on how to evacuate the airplane. Ask the flight attendant where child-size life preservers are stowed. If oxygen masks deploy, put on your mask first before helping the child. You won't be of any help if you succumb to hypoxia. Like adults, children should be restrained whenever they are seated.

Kids Traveling Alone

Tell your child what to expect during the flight, especially if this is her first trip alone. Discuss appropriate behavior and instruct her to obey the pilots and flight attendants at all times. However, do not impart any fears or phobias. Kids feel a mixture of elation, independence, insecurity and fear at being let loose from mom and dad's watchful eye. The last thing they need to see is anxiety in your face as you see them off at the gate. Always arrange for a responsible adult to meet your child at the destination.

Request that your child be seated in a row without other passengers. If the flight is full, request a seat that is not next to adults consuming alcohol. Introduce your child to one or more flight attendants so they know she is traveling alone.

Some people think it's okay for children to have multi-stage flights. Any time there is a need to change planes, though, there is a chance she could be stranded. Mechanical problems, adverse weather, ATC delays or other events may cause your child to miss the connection. Even if her connecting flight is operated by the same airline, don't risk sending her on her own. If, after landing at the intermediate stop, the airplane has a maintenance problem, the airline might change aircraft or transfer passengers to another airline. Rather than risk traumatizing your child, I suggest you never let her travel alone unless the flight is non-stop between departure and destination.

Having said that, even a non-stop flight may be diverted to an alternate airport due to bad weather or operational problem. The airline staff will ensure your child is catered to and put on a continuing flight to her original destination. If you have questions regarding airline policies, don't hesitate to ask.

Storms

Thunderstorms are extremely perilous to flying. Doppler radar on the ground, airborne weather radar and wind shear devices aboard jetliners, however, provide excellent images for pilots to avoid trouble.

The hazards of thunderstorms are violent winds, hail, lightning and severe turbulence. An extreme danger to aircraft taking off or landing is the " microburst," severe downdrafts from a single cell of a thunderstorm that reach speeds of hurricane force. Formerly a serious cause of accidents, the microburst is no longer a threat, thanks to effective detection systems.

If pilots avoid storms by flying around them, moderate turbulence may still be encountered. Heavy rain and hail can cause jet engines to stall or decelerate below idle speed. Pilots are highly trained to counter such situations.

If there are storms in the vicinity of the airport, the crew may decide not take off or land. When the flight is delayed or diverted, rest assured the storm will pass quickly. Pilots and FAA authorities determine when safe operation may be resumed.

If the captain is diverting around a storm, my advice is: Make sure your seat belt and that of your child are fastened tightly around your hip area. You may be in sunshine, but the turbulence can extend beyond the dark clouds.

St. Elmo's Fire

Often encountered near thunderstorms, St. Elmo's Fire is an eerie blue light emanating from sharp points and edges of the aircraft. The source is static electricity generated when flying through clouds, precipitation or dust. Although it can cause radio static, normal aircraft functions are unaffected. If you are lucky enough to see St. Elmo's fire, don't worry---just marvel at the wonders of nature.

Lightning

The most common form of lightning discharges bolts inside the same cloud. The bolt is not clearly distinguishable but appears as a broad flash across the sky. Lightning between clouds, on the other hand, is usually visible as bold flashes or strokes.

The FAA reports that commercial airplanes are struck by lightning on the average of once a year. In fact, airplanes build up an electrical charge when passing through clouds, which can trigger lightning strikes. Designers build airplanes to absorb and disperse lightning charges to neutralize their power. There is only one confirmed case of an airliner lost because of a lightning strike and that occurred almost 40 years ago.

Each part of an airplane is electrically bonded to the next so if any part of the airframe is struck by lightning, the charge travels through the conductive layer of the aircraft's skin and exits an extremity, such as the tail. Aircraft that use composite (plastic) materials instead of aluminum are fitted with a layer of conductive fibers or screens to carry lightning currents. In aircraft of all types, lightning shouldn't cause problems other than superficial scorching or pitting on the outside.

If you are aboard an aircraft struck by lightning, you may hear a loud noise and see a flash. But you need not worry. Airliners are rigorously tested to verify safety of the design. Surge protection devices are installed in electrical systems and wires shielded to prevent lightning currents from affecting sensitive computers and instruments. Pipes, fuel lines, access doors, filler caps and vents are also tested to withstand lightning strikes. The skin surrounding fuel tanks in each wing is thick enough to withstand lightning burning through and igniting fuel.

While each airplane is struck about once a year, your odds against being there at that time are high. I have been flying regularly for 25 years and can count on one hand the number of times my aircraft has been struck by lightning. On each occasion, there was no damage to the airplane.

Ice

Ice accumulating on an airplane degrades its lift and has caused catastrophic accidents. As little as 0.8 millimeters on an upper wing can increase drag and reduce lift by 25 percent. In winter, snow, sleet, fog, freezing drizzle and ice pellets cause ice to form on the airplane.

If ice is encountered in flight pilots usually have the time and airspace to respond. The most critical time is when the aircraft is taking off and climbing. Since 1968 there have been ten airline takeoff accidents in which ice contamination was a significant contributing factor.

The most memorable was an Air Florida B-737 that crashed into the Potomac River 37 seconds after take off from the nation's capital. Americans sat transfixed to their television screens in 1982 as rescuers desperately pulled freezing survivors out of the river. Investigators determined that the captain's inexperience with winter operations, and his failure to de-ice the airplane a second time before takeoff probably led to the disaster.

Tragedies like these lead to improvements. Aviation authorities, manufacturers and airlines join resources and develop systems to assure that similar accidents will not occur in the future.

If you are on an airplane in winter and the weather outside is cold and wet, pilots and ground crews coordinate to de-ice the airplane. Glycol solutions are sprayed onto wings and other surfaces as close as possible to pushback time.

Even the most effective anti-icing liquid, which prevents ice from building up again, loses effectiveness in less than 45 minutes. If the aircraft is stuck in line, waiting for takeoff more than about 20 minutes, a pilot, may walk back through the cabin to inspect the wings. He may elect to return the aircraft to the gate and be de-iced again. On more than one occasion, flight attendants and/or passengers have noticed snow and ice forming on the wings and brought it to the crew's attention.

One thing you need in winter is patience. If you are departing or arriving an airport with frequent episodes of bad weather, such as Minneapolis or Detroit, the airport will have equipment and personnel to deal with snow and ice in a timely manner. If it's an airport that does not suffer significant bouts of bad weather, such as Charlotte, NC, it may take longer.

Low Visibility

Fog, which is a cloud on the ground, is composed of water droplets or ice crystals. It reduces forward visibility, one of the most common weather hazards to pilots. Encounters with fog most often occur at coastal airports where moisture is abundant but it can form almost anywhere. Your jetliner has instruments that allow pilots to take off and land when visibility is extremely low, but there will be an occasional condition where visibility is just too poor.

Another hazard of fog is operating the aircraft on the ground. There have been nasty accidents when pilots lost their way while taxing. In the mid 1990s, a DC-9 collided with a B-727 taking off at Detroit. The DC-9 captain lost his way in heavy fog and taxied onto the active runway. Investigators concluded that miscommunication between the pilots and the absence of ground radar were contributing factors.

There is an intense effort to eliminate all of these low-visibility accidents. More airports are equipped with surface radar that tracks taxiing aircraft and warns of imminent collision. And the next generation of jetliners will have "synthetic vision" to give the pilot electronic eyes that pierce the densest fog and display a clear image of the runway and surrounding terrain.

Mid-Air Collisions

The most spectacular accident in aviation is the mid-air collision. In this event, two airplanes are involved and there are usually no survivors. The worst tragedy in airline history, in fact, was a collision between two B-747's in the Canary Islands. Fog shrouded the airport, as one airplane taxied on the runway. Because of a mix-up in communications, the second airplane unwittingly took off on the same runway and smashed into the one on the ground.

The breaking point over collisions happened when two airliners were cruising over the Grand Canyon nearly 50 years ago. One theory is that the airplanes converged while giving the passengers a good view of the natural wonder below. The accident initiated a major overhaul of the air traffic control system, equipping it with a new generation of surveillance radar. Earlier radar was a product of World War II, capable of showing aircraft only as crude "blips". By the late 1950's, airliners were equipped with transponders, a device which delivers a strong radar image, plus other information such as aircraft ID, speed and altitude. Air traffic controllers could now separate traffic much more reliably.

Although collisions were sharply reduced, the rare mid-airs that still occurred garnered such dramatic headlines that aviation authorities were pressured to provide another level of protection. The result is TCAS, for Traffic Alert and Collision Avoidance System. It is now aboard all commercial airliners.

TCAS is a remarkable device that senses nearby airplanes, tracks them in every dimension and delivers a warning to the pilot. If the threat grows serious, TCAS issues commands to the pilot to fly up or down to avoid a conflict.

The next generation of collision avoidance began development during the 1990's and, when completed, will cover aircraft of all sizes and types, in the air and on the ground. GPS and communications satellites will not only keep traffic safely separated, but allow pilots greater choice of routes to shorten the trip and reduce headwinds.

Chapter 12

Martial Arts

If you would like to advance your martial art skills, I encourage you to join a club. Consider the guidelines described below and pick carefully before committing yourself.

Martial Arts: *What Are They?*

Any fighting method is basically a martial art. Common myths about Karate and other martial arts claim that practitioners defend against sudden attacks without suffering so much as a glancing blow, that size does not matter, that techniques against knife attacks leave the martial artist unscathed and that each style is better than the other. Not one of these claims is true.

A surprise attack means a person is not expecting the first blow. By definition, he or she will be hit at least once. Common sense dictates that size always matters. This does not mean a smaller person cannot overcome a larger adversary, but the greater physical strength of the larger person means that if the smaller person is hit, more damage is done. When defending against knife attacks, many procedures call for deflecting knife thrusts. There's no guarantee you will not be cut, but the object is to stop lethal penetration to the body.

As for one style being better than the other, in my mind, any style that concentrates on practical techniques is superior to methods that rely on your partner complying with rules of engagement. In mounting an aggressive defense, I advocate doing whatever is necessary to disable an opponent, based on the theory that your opponent is intent on doing the same.

Training in martial arts increases your conditioning and reflexes; in a surprise attack you respond better than the untrained person. You are more attuned to aggression and anticipate threats earlier. Keep in mind, however, that the element of surprise has been used for centuries by attackers because it gives a strong advantage.

Boxing versus Karate

Traditional Karate practitioners fight by keeping their center of gravity close to the ground. They use kicks, knees, elbows and other techniques aimed at sensitive body areas and pressure points. This is illegal in the art of boxing. Karate practitioners do not lean into their punches but depend on their legs, buttocks and upright body to power their strikes. Because they don't wear protective gloves, Karate fighters learn to punch with precision, using one or two knuckles of the hand. Unlike boxers, they attempt to sweep their opponent off his feet, then follow the adversary to the ground to continue an aggressive defense. Boxers will dance around their opponent and offer a profile target, while Karate practitioners do not move around as much and adopt a stance that offers their opponent a better target.

Judo

Practitioners of Judo immobilize their opponent by grappling them to the floor and locking their joints. They keep their distance by techniques designed to disable the opponent in the first exchange. Judo has close ties to Greek wrestling and Sumo, and is more sport-oriented than Karate.

Aikido

Far more traditional than the martial arts just described, Aikido artists engage in spiritual, even religious, rituals. Like new-age proponents, Aikido practitioners believe the body has an energy force – *Ki* – that can be harnessed to increase power. It requires close-in techniques to allow the practitioner to bring an opponent down heavily. Karate fighters, on the other hand, maintain distance from their opponent until he has been weakened by kicks, punches and other techniques.

Ju-Jitsu

This martial art was used for combat by samurai in unarmed defense on the battlefield. It relies on using an opponent's strength and momentum against him and includes defenses against armed attackers. Judo and Aikido are modern-day derivatives of Ju-Jitsu. Karate uses close-in techniques, but relies on aggressive strikes administered while perfectly distanced from an opponent.

Tae Kwon Do

A Korean martial art, Tae Kwon Do relies more on kicking. As a result, artists adopt a high, mobile stance and use hands and arms mostly for protection against attack. Karate fighters rely more on punching and other hand techniques, while using the feet for low kicks and leg sweeps. As a result, Karate practitioners adopt solid footing stances and generally do not use high kicks unless they stand on an extremely sound surface.

Tai Chi

This ancient Chinese art relies on slow, smooth motions to increase the practitioner's focus, relaxation and serenity. Karate is more aggressive and violent and increases athleticism rather than inner harmony. Tai Chi is more a meditative, than a fighting, art.

Kung Fu

There is no ancient Chinese art called "Kung Fu." Rather, it is a western expression to describe many colorful Chinese martial art practices. Karate, being Japanese-based, is more pragmatic, while Kung Fu is typically theatrical. That does not mean that Kung Fu techniques are not extremely effective, just that it is more flamboyant than Karate.

Muay Thai Kickboxing

This ancient Thai martial art is irritating and exciting to watch. Bouts in Thailand are filled with loud music, dancing and singing. Practitioners use any part of the body to strike an opponent except their head. Head kicks, knees and elbows are preferred in lieu of punching, which is considered a weaker offensive tactic. Some Karate styles embrace techniques from other martial arts, such as my own Zen Do Kai club, and incorporate knee and elbow techniques used in Muay Thai Kickboxing .

There are many other forms of martial art from around the world based on the history of the region. If you intend to join a club, the selection of styles is large. Look for is a club that includes "freestyle" in its claims of effectiveness.

Zen Do Kai

Any martial art practiced diligently becomes a way of life and changes your development as an individual. This is summed up in the mission statement of Zen Do Kai:

> Through the martial arts, create opportunities for individuals to exceed their limitations and reach their maximum potential, physically, mentally, and spiritually so they become a better person.

Since the 1960s, Bob Jones (not the American religious leader) has become synonymous with the Australian security industry and martial arts community. For the last forty years, Bob's

Bob Jones, founder of Zen Do Kai, holds the rank of Sichi Dan (7th Dan). One of the highest ranking martial artists in Australia, he was awarded the Blitz Martial Arts Magazine Lifetime Achievement Award.

Zen Do Kai clubs, based in Australia and New Zealand, have taught thousands of men, women and children the art of self defense.

Zen Do Kai is a freestyle, dynamic martial art. It is freestyle in that it borrows from martial arts all over the world, and dynamic as its techniques change to meet the current environment. Although Zen Do Kai has roots in traditional Karate, it has been modified to exclude impractical techniques and include effective practices from other styles, such as Muay Thai Boxing. This includes locks and holds, throws, vital point striking, grappling, boxing, and kick boxing. Traditional Karate forms and weaponry are also included in Zen Do Kai training, the latter for advanced students.

Bob introduced the Freefighting Forms And Self Defense Tournaments (FAST) to all Zen Do Kai dojos to improve the members' abilities through heavy competition. I competed in several club tournaments in Brisbane and won the privilege of wearing a yellow jersey bearing the number two, representing my wins.

Zen Do Kai black belts began to be employed for security at major rock concerts from the seventies. Bob himself, acted as personal body guard for such rock stars such as the Rolling Stones, Fleetwood Mac, ABBA, David Bowie, Boy George and Linda Rondstat. There are about 1,000 Zen Do Kai schools of self defense throughout Australasia, with 20,000 students training towards their black belt.

Join a Club

If you want to advance your skills in self defense, visit local clubs, assess whether you think the style is practical and make the decision based on your personal needs.

Some parents hesitate to allow their kids to study martial arts because they think the child may become violent or, worse, be hurt. On the contrary, Zen Do Kai and other martial arts require rigorous training and dedication. Kids who want to learn to "beat somebody up" drop out after the first few weeks. All martial arts demand strict moral codes of conduct. Kids who stay the course learn how to defend themselves against multiple attackers and this knowledge builds self esteem and confidence. The result is that kids are *less* likely to get into scraps when they know they would come out the winner.

As for getting hurt during training, most clubs allow only light contact in junior ranks. Teachers encourage students to wear safety equipment, such as shin and foot pads, cups and mouthguards in case an opponent loses control. Some clubs spar with full contact but, as you might expect, only advanced students train in this manner and only when suited up with padding.

Whatever the case, club teachers keep a close eye on the safety of *all* members, especially children. The aim of martial arts is personal development, not personal destruction. Don't hesitate to join a club yourself and sign up your kids. They will thank you for years to come and, if you train together, you will have a family activity everyone can enjoy.

Appendix A

Flight Crew Training

Airline crews go through rigorous training before they qualify to operate commercial aircraft. Most already have considerable experience in general aviation or the military. Pilots join an airline's seniority list and receive the rank of second or first officer, depending on the aircraft they will fly.

Over several months, there is classroom instruction, simulator practice and flying experience. At the end of training, proficiency is determined by an FAA check airman. Every following year, pilots receive line checks during normal flights. On top of this, twice a year, each pilot undergoes simulator checking and training. During these sessions, many emergency and abnormal conditions are practiced in the flight simulator.

Most airlines also include a yearly simulator session to enhance crew cooperation. These sessions, called Line Oriented Flight Training (LOFT), generally present pilots with problems compounded by other challenges such as bad weather. Pilots have no idea what they may encounter during a LOFT session. In the debrief, pilots critique their individual and group performance.

Flight Attendants
Although flight attendants try to assure that every passenger has a comfortable flight, their primary duty is to follow safety regulations and lead passengers during an emergency. Flight attendants are typically briefed before each flight by the captain; he or she relays circumstances that affect the trip such as flight time, route and cruise

altitude. This helps flight attendants answer passenger questions.

Flight attendant training begins with 4 to 7 weeks of instruction. Recruits learn emergency procedures in the classroom and practice evacuations in an airline mock-up. They learn how to guide passengers on emergency actions, such as how to adopt a brace position. First aid, water survival and how to deal with disruptive passengers are covered. Aircraft door-opening and slide rafts that fail to inflate automatically are practiced. Hijack scenarios are discussed and flight attendants usually watch a video on actions to take during a hijack. Until recently, hijack procedures were based historical experience .

Flight regulations, dangerous goods and other topics are given before flight attendants are released for training on actual flights. A flight attendant is then checked for proficiency and released to fly the line. They are periodically checked on regular flights to be sure that standards are maintained.

Yearly Refresher

Pilots and flight attendants take yearly emergency training. Large airlines have mock-ups of airplane interiors and cockpits. Small airlines send their crews to larger airline training facilities or professional crew training companies. For 8 to 12 hours, pilots and flight attendants are instructed on emergency equipment, cabin door emergency opening, evacuation, ditching drills and hijacks. Some training includes hands-on practice. Pilots and flight attendants may form groups to discuss timely subjects, recent accidents and other areas to enlighten everyone's knowledge of what is going on in the industry.

Active Response

Before September 11, pilots and flight attendants were taught to respond passively to a hijacking and expect the episode to end without violence. Whether threatened by a mentally-unstable passenger or politically-motivated zealot, history taught that complying with their demands resulted in fewest casualties.

Since the September 11 attacks, airlines scrambled to revise training programs to help crews overcome suicidal hijackers. In my view, training should be amended to include self-defense instruction, conflict resolution and improvisation. This would mean an extra day or two of training every year, but circumstances deem this necessary.

Self defense Program

I believe that training for crew members should be conducted in groups of about 25 for 6 to 8 hours. Pilots and flight attendants would attend, dressed in sweat suits and sneakers. The day may be organized in the following manner:

9:00 to 10:30 – Classroom

Receive written and verbal information on company policies and procedures in the event of hijacking. The material is presented by instructors, followed by open discussion.

10:30 to 10:45 – Break

10:45 to 12:00: Video Presentation

Videos show self defense techniques to be learned. Instructors stress the importance of each technique. Open discussion follows of points not covered in the videos.

12:00 to 1:00: Lunch

1:00 to 2:45: Gym

Gymnasium or large room with mirrored wall.

Crew members split into pairs for ten minutes of warm-up exercises. Self defense techniques shown on video are demonstrated by instructors and each pair of crew members practice the technique, first as defender, then as attacker. Instructors determine that each crew member has a grasp of techniques.

2:45 to 3:00: Break

3:00 to 4:45: Aircraft mock-up

Crew members relocate to the airline's mock-up training facility where flight attendants and pilots divide into groups. One instructor reviews techniques with flight attendants in the mock-up cabin, while another does the same for pilots, but in the cockpit. When each crew member is satisfied that he or she understands the self defense techniques, instructors dress in heavily padded clothing and act as assailants in improvised hijacking scenarios.

Flight attendants and pilots split into normal crew-size groups during this period. While one crew is improvising, others observe. Scenarios cover materials presented previously, but culminate in crew members defending themselves and overcoming hijackers. At the end of each episode, crew members constructively critique the team's performance. I recommend that training improvisations are as realistic as possible, with hijackers armed with mock weapons.

3:45 to 4:30: Critique

Crew members critique the training program and write down complaints or suggestions. Crew members then hit the showers and sign off.

Appendix B

Chronology of Hijacking

Terrorism has been around since biblical times, but with the coming of the aviation industry a new channel of murderous rage became available. Terrorists over the past fifty years mostly planned to bring down airplanes by planting explosives on board. But using the airplane as a missile, as done on September 11, is a new phenomenon.

The only comparison is when a pilot flew a World War II bomber into the Empire State Building in 1947. But it hardly was an act of terrorism. The pilot was lost in fog over Manhattan, an unthinkable event today, thanks to tremendous advances in air traffic control. But it has some bearing on September 11 because it encouraged engineers to design the World Trade Center to withstand the impact of a Boeing 707.

The Heritage Foundation Center for Data Analysis reports there were 103 air hijacking incidents in US-registered aircraft from 1975 to 2001. During the same period, there were 439 hijackings of foreign-registered aircraft.

From 1995 to 2000, seventy-seven Americans were killed and 651 wounded in international terrorist attacks. But Americans at home were free from attack by foreign zealots. All that changed on September 11. Following are brief outlines of some of the most violent terrorist attacks in the last fifty years:

September 9, 1949

In Quebec, Canada a bomb exploded in the forward cargo compartment of a Canadian Pacific DC-3 killing 23 people.

November 1, 1955

Near Denver, Colorado a United Airlines DC-6 crashed after a bomb planted by a relative of one of the passengers exploded in flight – 44 people died.

July 25, 1957

Over Daggett, California a bomb exploded in the aft lavatory of a Western Airlines CV-240. The pilots managed to land the aircraft safely; however, one person was killed by the blast.

January 6, 1960

A National Airlines DC-6 crashed near Bolivia, North Carolina after a bomb exploded while the aircraft was cruising at 18,000 feet. All 34 people on board were killed.

May 22, 1962

After a bomb explosion a Continental Airlines Boeing 707 crashed near Unionville, Missouri killing 45 passengers and crew.

May 7, 1964

A suicide killer shot both pilots aboard a Pacific Airline's Fairchild F-27 in flight. The aircraft crashed near Oakland, California and all 44 people onboard perished.

July 8, 1965

After a supposed sabotage act, a Canadian Pacific DC-6 collided with another aircraft and crashed in British Columbia, Canada with the death of all 52 people onboard.

September 16, 1970

Five separate PLO hijackers attacked five jetliners in unison. Sky marshals killed one hijacker and disarmed one bomb.

January 23, 1971

A hijacker forced Korean Airlines F-27 pilots to crash-land near the North Korean border in South Korea. He later killed himself with a hand grenade, killing two other people in the process. Fifty-eight passengers and crew survived.

May 8, 1972

Hijackers with guns attacked a Sabena jetliner, killing one person and injuring 4 others.

May 30, 1972

Just 22 days after the Sabena hijack, in a horrific act, terrorists sprayed people in the airport lounge at the Ben Gurion International Airport in Israel with automatic weapons, killing 26 and injuring another 76 people.

On the *same* day an El Al airplane had a bomb explode in its baggage compartment, but no one was injured due to the company having armored aircraft compartments. (Armoring baggage compartments is garnering serious talk in America's campaign to improve air safety.)

September 5, 1972

In retaliation for the failed bombing of the El Al airplane mentioned above, and for Israeli acts of reprisals, 11 Israeli athletes in the Olympic Village in Munich were attacked and killed by terrorists.

October 1972

A Lufthansa jetliner was hijacked but, fortunately, no injuries resulted.

April 1973

A crew member and a suicide bomber aboard an Aeroflot flight were killed when the bomb went off during a struggle.

July 20, 1973

An explosion onboard a hijacked Japan Airlines airplane killed one person and injured another.

August 5, 1973

Five people were killed and 55 injured in a rescue attempt gone awry after a TWA flight was forced by hijackers to land in Athens, Greece.

December 1973

Four months later, the same group hijacked a Lufthansa jetliner, but fortunately no one was injured.

Five days later…

A PanAm airliner was taken over on the ground and the customs area attacked, resulting in 30 deaths and 28 injuries.

February 20, 1974

Hijackers exploded a bomb onboard an Air Vietnam airplane killing 3 people and injuring 6 others.

August 6, 1974

Seventeen people were seriously injured and two people died after a bomb exploded near the PanAm ticket counter in Terminal 2 at Los Angeles International.

September 8, 1974

Following what NTSB officials believed to be an inflight bomb explosion in the aft cargo compartment, a TWA Boeing 707 crashed into the Ionian Sea near Greece, killing all onboard.

June 3, 1975

A small bomb exploded onboard an aircraft (undisclosed), causing rapid decompression. Fourteen people were injured and two killed, including the hijacker.

May 23, 1976

After what officials hoped would be a peaceful end to a hostage situation onboard a Philippine Airline BAC 1-11 at Zamboanga Airport, Mindanao, Philippines, hijackers opened fire with guns and hand grenades, killing 13 people.

June 27, 1976

Air France flight 139 carrying a large number of Israeli citizens was hijacked by PLO terrorists and forced to land at Entebbe Airport in Uganda. Israeli commandos later rescued hostages in a spectacular raid that resulted in only 4 deaths other than the terrorists.

July 2, 1976

A hijacker detonated a bomb onboard an Eastern Airlines flight but no person was injured other than the hijacker who died in the blast.

December 4, 1977

The crew on a Malaysian Airlines Boeing 737 attempted to overpower a hijacker who then detonated the bomb he was carrying. The midair explosion resulted in the deaths of all 100 people on the aircraft.

August 18, 1978

A hijacker exploded the bomb he was carrying onboard a Philippine Airlines flight killing himself and injuring 3 others, including one crew member.

August 11, 1982

A passenger was killed when a bomb under his seat exploded on a PanAm Boeing 747 near Hawaii.

June 23, 1985

An Air India Boeing-747 enroute from Toronto, Canada to Bombay, India broke up in flight after a bomb exploded onboard. Aircraft pieces fell into the Atlantic Ocean near the Irish Coast. All 329 people onboard lost their lives.

December 27, 1985

In Rome's Leonardo da Vinci Airport, four terrorists opened fire with automatic weapons and hand grenades at the check-in areas of El Al, TWA and PanAm. Fourteen people were killed, including 3 of the terrorists. Seventy people were wounded the same day.

At Vienna's Schwechat Airport, three terrorists opened fire with automatic weapons and hand grenades on passengers in the El Al lounge. Three persons were killed, including one of the terrorists. Another 47 people were injured.

April 2, 1986

Following a bomb explosion onboard a TWA Boeing-727 near Athens, Greece a hole was blown in the fuselage causing four people to be sucked out of the aircraft. Pilots landed the aircraft safely following the deaths of the four passengers.

September 6, 1986

A PanAm 747 with 375 passengers and crew was held hostage in Karachi Airport, Pakistan. During a rescue attempt, 21 people died from gunfire and hand grenade shrapnel.

December 25, 1986

An inflight gun battle between hijackers and security personnel on an Iraqi Airlines 737 resulted in an unsuccessful forced landing in Saudi Arabia. Seventy-one people died and 36 survived the event.

December 7, 1987

Near Paso Robles, California a Pacific Southwest Bae 146 jet crashed with all 43 people losing their lives. A disgruntled ex-employee had shot and killed both pilots. This act was imitated by a disgruntled Fedex employee several years later. He attempted to kill all three pilots of a DC-10 with a hammer.

December 21, 1988

Over Lockerbie, Scotland a PanAm 747 exploded in midair when a bomb, later found to have been hidden in a radio, detonated. All 259 people were killed in the crash that followed and 11 Lockerbie residents killed by falling debris.

September 19, 1989

A French UTA DC-10 jetliner exploded in flight from a bomb onboard and crashed in the Tenere Desert in Niger. All 171 people onboard were killed.

October 2, 1990

In a multi-aircraft collision, a Xiamen Airlines 737 careened off the runway during an emergency landing. A hijacker struggling with the pilots caused the aircraft to hit a China Southwest Airlines 707 and, ricocheting off this airplane, slammed into a China Southern Airline 757. As a result, 132 people died, but 141 survived; 20 from the Boeing-737 and 71 in the Boeing-757.

August 28, 1993

Eighty-two people died after a hijacker forced a Tajikistan Airlines Yak-40 pilot to attempt an overweight takeoff. The plane overran the runway and fell down a river bank.

March 1996

A hijacker with a gun and bomb seized control of a Turkish Cypriot plane departing Cyprus for Istanbul, Turkey. All people onboard were freed after the hijacker surrendered to authorities in Munich, Germany.

June 1997

An Air Malta jet enroute to Istanbul, Turkey was hijacked by two men who claimed to have a bomb. After landing in Cologne, Germany the men gave themselves up to authorities. There were no bombs found onboard.

February 1998

A hijacker claiming to be hiding a bomb in a teddy bear seized control of a Turkish Airlines plane shortly after it took off from Adana Airport in Turkey. Security agents disguised as caterers arrested the man after landing, while all 41 crew and passengers were still onboard. No explosives were found.

October 1998

Another Turkish Airlines flight was hijacked after taking off from Adana Airport. The hijacker, who demanded to be flown to Switzerland, was killed by elite anti-terrorist soldiers after the airplane landed in Ankara, Turkey for a supposed fuel stop. No passengers or crew were injured.

October 1999

An Egyptian jetliner was seized by a man armed with a knife after it departed Istanbul, Turkey. He was convinced by the pilots that a fuel stop would be required for the airplane to make it to his requested destination, London. Authorities in Hamburg, Germany arrested the man after landing. No passengers or crew were hurt.

February 10, 2001

In a bizarre incident, a policeman shot two of his colleagues to death, wounded two others then turned the gun on himself near the immigration counter in Calcutta, India.. Fortunately, British Airways passengers had just cleared the area.

March 15 and 16, 2001

A Vnukovo Airlines TU-154 was seized by Chechnyan terrorists after it took off from Istanbul on a scheduled flight to Moscow. The plane was diverted to Medina Airport in Saudi Arabia, where 60 passengers were released. During the hijackers' attack, the plane dropped 10,000 feet as a passenger valiantly fought them from entering the cockpit. After 18 hours of non-successful negotiations, Saudi special forces stormed the aircraft and freed 175 passengers and crew. Three people, a hijacker, a passenger and a flight attendant, died in the assault.

Conclusions

From these incidents I have four observations:

1. German authorities have an admirable record of negotiating peaceful resolutions to hijack situations. Perhaps American authorities should consult with their German counterparts and benchmark their strategies.

2. The PanAm 747 that crashed in Lockerbie instigated a study to fortify cargo compartments against bomb damage. To date, no aircraft manufacturer or airline, other than El Al, followed through with bomb-proofing their airplanes.

3. One of two most probable future attacks could come from terrorists walking into an airport and spraying passengers with automatic weapon fire and hand grenades. Police and national guards need to cover every major airport to protect against such an event.

4. The second most probable attack is from a bomb exploding in an airport or on a flight. Although Transportation Secretary Norman Mineta stated that he would like accelerated installation of explosive-sensing scanners at all 420 commercial US airports (currently at 132), this process will take time.

Appendix C

Airplane Exits

The floor plans beginning on the next page cover most airliners. The locations of exits usually don't vary during the life of an airplane, but be sure to check the safety card on your flight to positively identify where exits are located. Also, look around after you are seated to locate the nearest exit. It's also a good idea to look for the next farthest exit in case the primary one becomes blocked. When you are seated, count the number of seats to the exit. In the event of lowered visibility in the cabin, that number may help find your way.

Airbus A-300

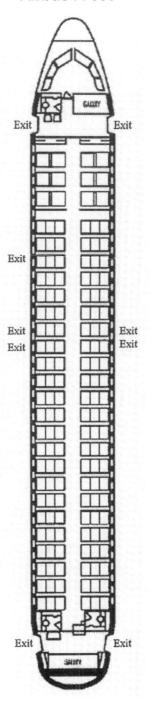

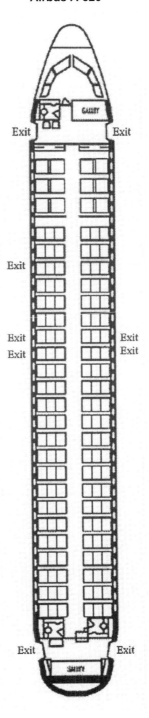

Airbus A-320

ATR-42

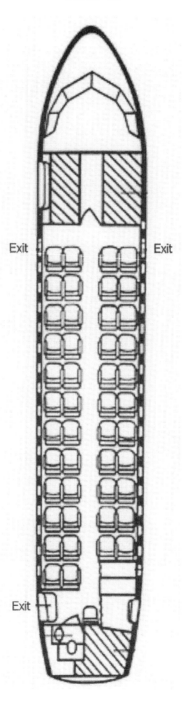

Exit   Exit

Exit

ATR-72

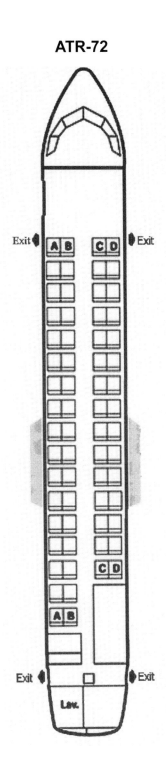

B-727

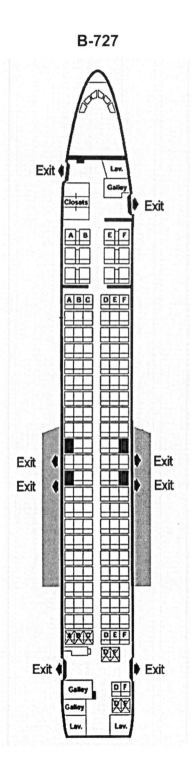

B-737

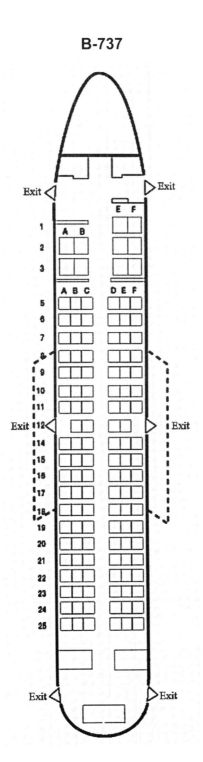

B-747

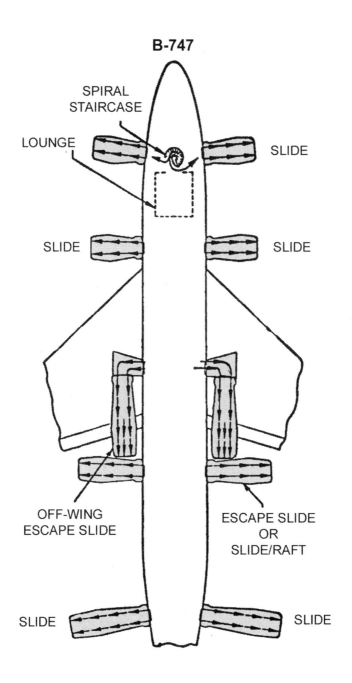

SPIRAL STAIRCASE

LOUNGE

SLIDE

SLIDE

SLIDE

OFF-WING ESCAPE SLIDE

ESCAPE SLIDE OR SLIDE/RAFT

SLIDE

SLIDE

B-1900

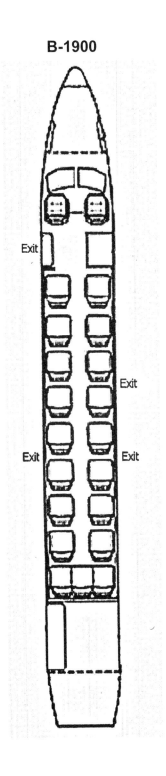

DC-9

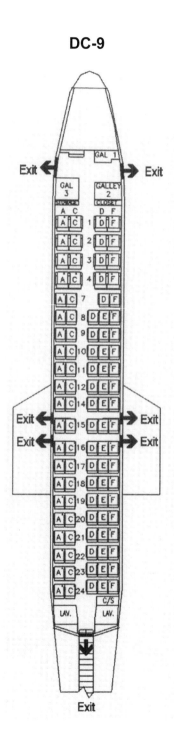

DHC-8

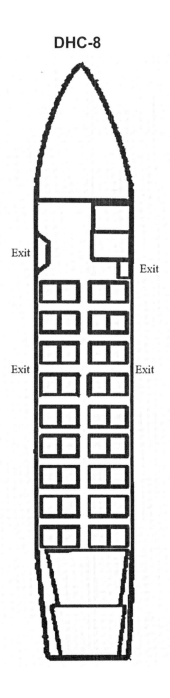

EMB-145

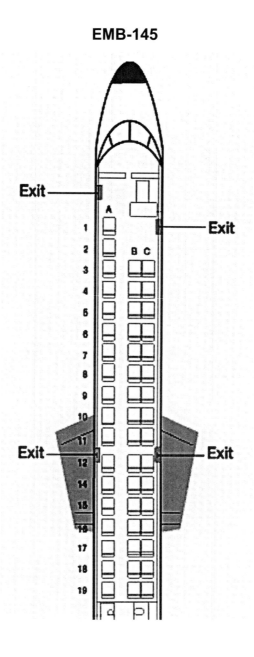

F-100

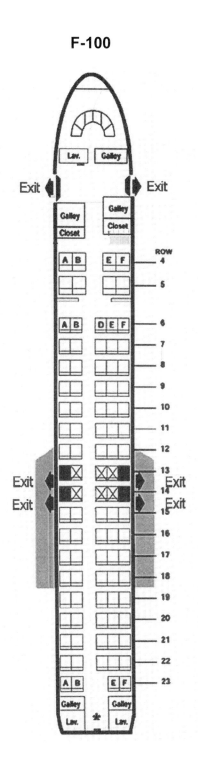

Jetstream-3100

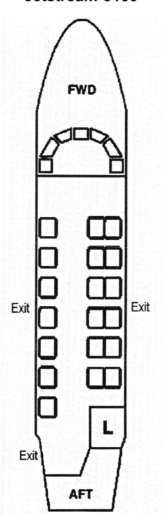

175

Jetstream-4100

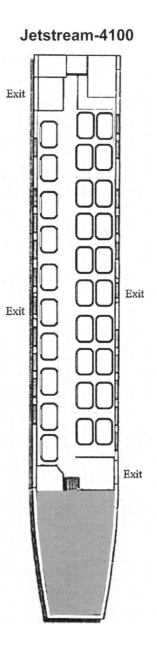

MD-80

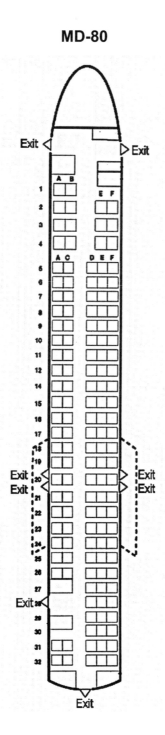

MD-82

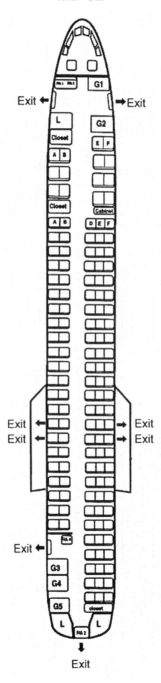

MD-88

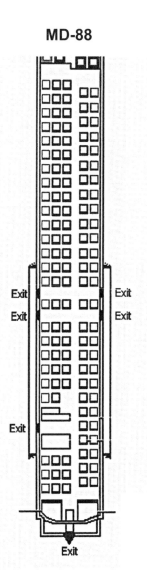

Regional Jet

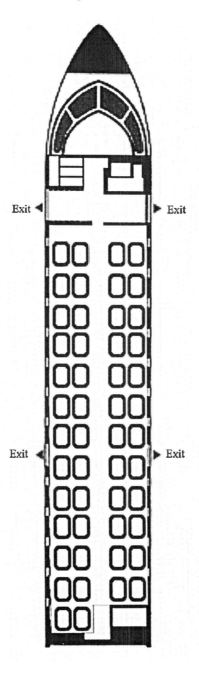

S-340

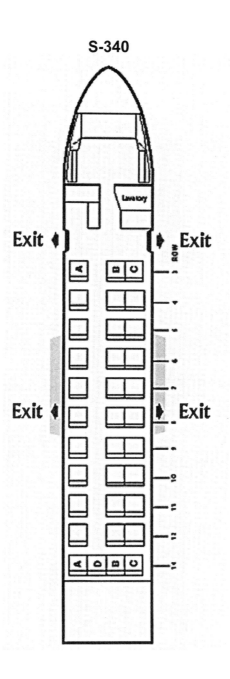

About the Author

Ken Cubbin, born in Sydney, Australia, brings a remarkable combination of talents to this book. He's flown over 30 years for major airlines as a flight engineer and training instructor. He's researched safety issues facing flight crews flying complex airliners.

At the same time, Ken earned a coveted Black Belt in Karate and pursued a sportsman's interest in small arms. Little did he realize that the tragic events of September 11 would draw him to the problem of helplessness in airline passengers in time of crisis. This book---empowering the flying public to fight back---is his response, as he relates in his own words;

I joined Qantas in the 1970's as an apprentice aircraft technician in the airlines' Golden Age. I not only expected a job for life, but benefits and salary the envy of other industries. At the end of my first tenure, I was promoted to ground school instructor, a welcome stepping stone to getting off the 'floor'.

After applying for flight engineer for what seemed an eternity, I received a call from TransAustralia Airlines (TAA). Two weeks later I was in the flight engineer course .

While living in Melbourne I became interested in martial arts and joined the local Zen Do Kai club. I savored not only the physical training, but the psychological benefits. Proficiency in self defense is a great confidence booster. Within a few years I earned the rank of brown belt. Then, TAA transferred me to its Brisbane base.

Training in the Zen Do Kai club in Brisbane differed from what I learned in Melbourne. Instead of a traditional approach, the style was more like street-fighting. For example, my *sensei* – teacher –was fond of saying, "Spinning kicks won't help when you are on the street wearing leather-soled shoes and standing in gravel. You'll end up on your arse." He advocated short kicks to keep a person's center of gravity low. Not pretty, but effective.

I listened carefully. He had the aura of one who knew the subject first hand. He also taught kick boxing and I participated in that sport with vigor. He asked me one night whether I was interested in training to fight in the ring. I wasn't, but felt honored he thought me proficient enough. Within two years, I was ready for black belt grading. At least, I thought I was.

Black belt grading consists of one hundred pushups, one hundred sit-ups, thirty spinning kicks and other techniques. I performed *katas* – attack and defense moves to heighten focus, demonstrate techniques and develop concentration. One *kata* is done with maximum effort to flex every muscle in the body. To maintain maximum tension, another black belt punched me full force in the stomach. The blow surprised club members watching, but I bore it well and was allowed to continue.

After *katas*, my *sensei* announced I would spar fifteen, three-minute rounds with members of the club. My first opponent was a young woman renown for flexibility. It was not uncommon to see her body pressed to a wall with one leg vertically above her head. As we sparred, my spinning wheel kick struck her hard in her breast. The crowd murmured. Striking a senior rank with such ferocity usually incurs the person's wrath. But in this case, she merely nodded to my mumbled apology.

After nine rounds, my endurance and accuracy were waning. In a bout with a brown belt, I misjudged distance and knocked him to the floor. I anxiously looked at my *sensei*--- he had the power to stop the grading for my transgression.

"I think he slipped *sensei*," I said.

He looked at the brown belt on the floor for any objection. Brown belt agreed he'd slipped, so the red welt on the brown belt's face was ignored and the bout continued.

I made the same slip, unfortunately, with a young black belt. I hit him hard in the face and he staggered. Instead of crying foul, he responded with a jumping front kick that hit my mid-section full force. I went down fast and lay there, unable to catch my breath. S*ensei* stood over me and shouted, "Shake it off! Get up or I'll end your grading right now!"

It took every ounce of strength to get off the floor and continue. But soon *sensi* announced I had completed fifteen rounds and I should squat on the floor to await his pronouncement.

After several minutes, he stood in front of me and said I would have to fight another five rounds! I was stunned. I had given my all and didn't have an ounce of strength left. I thought I had passed, so why fight more? I got to my feet.

"I think you know what these rounds are for," he said.

I was being given the chance, I realized, to earn the right to wear a black uniform – the sign of strength.

To this day I don't know how I completed those last five bouts, but I mustered the resolve to continue. I could barely feel my arms after defending myself from so many kicks and strikes. I fought from pure will and determination not to quit. And then, it was over.

I received the black belt that night and the right to wear a black uniform. With it came the privilege to bear a Bushido Cross ---the sign of the warrior.

My purpose in writing this book was to answer common questions and give you facts concerning aviation security. I have shown how you can defend yourself against terrorists and protect yourself in emergencies. In short, I have tried to give you back a sense of control. We must each make the decision that we will not rely on other people to protect us, for to do so will only increase our anxiety. We are not victims unless we choose to be.